THE DOMINANT MAN

The
Dominant Man

The Pecking Order in
Human Society

HUMPHRY KNIPE & GEORGE MACLAY

FONTANA/COLLINS

First published in Great Britain by Souvenir Press Ltd 1972
First published in Fontana 1973
Copyright © 1972 by Humphry Knipe and George Maclay

Made and printed in Great Britain by
Richard Clay (The Chaucer Press) Ltd
Bungay, Suffolk
for the Publishers Wm. Collins Sons & Co. Ltd,
14 St James's Place, London SW1

CONTENTS

CHAPTER I

ANIMAL DOMINANCE

The dominant man finds it easy to influence other people and to bend their wishes to suit his own. Women find him fascinating. He seems to exude a mysterious and compelling force that makes him the centre of attention at social gatherings. Wherever he goes, people are constantly looking at his face to see what sort of response he considers appropriate to the social situation. Recognition of his ability to take command and define the tone of a social gathering has given rise to such descriptive terms as *charisma*, *personal magnetism*, *high-power personality*. It has always been accepted that any man aspiring to the position of self-made leader will never succeed unless he possesses a magnetic social presence. This is believed by many people to be a rare and somehow superhuman quality which enables the powerful man to dazzle his contemporaries.

Research into the mechanics of human communication has made it possible to describe in detail how dominant people project their aura of command. Contrary to many popularly held beliefs, the dominant individual differs from others not so much by what he says but by the way he says it, and by the way he stands, walks, and acts.

History and anthropology demonstrate that all human societies are organized around some kind of dominance hierarchy, and clinical studies have shown that a human community can in fact be divided into three categories of personality: high dominance, low dominance, and middle dominance. Such studies indicate that each of these three basic personality types behaves in a characteristic way throughout all the affairs of daily life. The high dominance person can be most easily identified by the fact that he feels superior to others in a very general sense. He feels sure of his ability to manage other people. Characteristically, he never feels shy, timid, or embarrassed. At the other end of the scale, the low dominance person feels inferior in the company of most people. He does not think much of himself. Given a chance, he would rather be like somebody else.

Of course, all of us experience our own individual ups and downs. Quite naturally, we tend to think of our own familiar range of dominance feelings as covering the complete spectrum of possibilities. But in fact, experiments demonstrate that any one individual's fluctuation in dominance feelings usually covers only a small segment of the total scale of dominance feelings experienced throughout his community.

To what extent are our relationships with one another governed by these personal differences in dominance feeling? What connection exists between a feeling of dominance and social success? These are questions that can now be answered.

Many of the most important breakthroughs in the study of dominance have been made possible through the rapid expansion of the social sciences, social psychology, and sociology. The most interesting single source of data has almost certainly been social anthropology, since this field involves the study of personal prestige and formal rank in a worldwide assortment of what might be considered natural laboratories. In this first chapter, however, we shall confine ourselves to painting in the animal background against which human dominance must be viewed if we want to keep it in its proper biological perspective, and we shall begin by outlining the evolutionary foundations of personal influence and personal magnetism. For this we must turn to the little-known and comparatively new science of ethology.

To the layman, ethology is still a small name among the sciences; it was only recently that it made its appearance as an obscure subdivision of zoology. Initially, the ethologists confined themselves to comparing the inborn behaviour patterns of different animal species in an attempt to explain how these forms of behaviour had evolved. However, when they turned their sights on to the sacred subject of human behaviour, they found themselves rocketed to the front of the scientific limelight. In a matter of two or three decades, the ethologists have brought about a revolution in man's understanding of his social behaviour. The self-study of man inevitably remained vague and speculative for as long as he looked back at himself in splendid isolation, with nothing to compare himself against and without careful reference to his evolutionary background. Ethologists point out that many aspects of animal behaviour have obvious counterparts in human behaviour. Thanks to their work, it is now generally recognized that by drawing careful conclusions from the function and malfunction of animal behaviour patterns, man can gain valuable insights into the hidden and, at present, uncontrollable forces operating in his own communities.

At first, this radically new approach to the study of man met with a predictable storm of emotional opposition. Any openly profane treatment of human nature was bound to be hotly criticized. But during the last decade, growing numbers of social scientists have been won over to the ethological viewpoint and have begun to introduce the ethologist's new biological perspective into their own scientific disciplines. This trend has been accompanied by rapid progress in the detailed study of man's closest animal relatives in their wild state. Casual observations of animal behaviour in the wild by hunters and explorers are being replaced by a great bank of scientifically tested information. Already these developments have led to discoveries of central importance to the explanation of dominance. In particular, we now know that a type of dominance that can scarcely be distinguished from human dominance is characteristic of all socially organized birds and mammals.

In this introductory chapter, we shall summarize briefly some of the most important conclusions reached to date through the study of dominance in animal societies. We can safely promise at this stage that the ethologist's comparative approach to understanding man, as opposed to the overwhelmingly introspective approach of classical psychology, has brought an extraordinary insight into the nature of dominant and subordinate human personalities. By stripping interpersonal dominance of its magical, science-proof cloak, the ethologists have breached the most formidable taboo still at work in modern society. The demystification of dominance promises changes in our way of life at least as great as those brought by the demystification of sexual behaviour.

The Pecking Order System

The earliest scientific study of dominance in an animal society was carried out on domestic fowls by the Danish zoologist

Thorleif Schjelderup-Ebbe in 1913. Most of us take for granted the constant bickering and squabbling that seem to go on in every hen coop. Schjelderup-Ebbe took the trouble to find out what all this noise was about.

Initially Ebbe had noticed that one of his hens consistently tyrannized the rest of his flock and drove them away from choice pieces of food with a flurry of pecks. This made him curious about the whole social structure of the chicken run, and so he set about learning to identify every bird by its appearance and behaviour. Immediately a pattern emerged out of what had at first appeared to be random aggression.

In any squabble between two particular birds, the same one was always the aggressor and the other gave way without any significant degree of resistance. It soon became obvious to Schjelderup-Ebbe that his hen coop society had established a network of superior–inferior relationships in which every individual knew its proper place. He found that these relationships of dominance and subordination extended throughout the flock so that every bird except those at the top or the bottom of the ladder was dominant over some of its flockmates and subordinate to others.

Schjelderup-Ebbe appropriately described this social system as a *pecking order*. This term was subsequently adopted by zoologists and naturalists even when describing animals that assert their version of status-aggression by butting, biting, scratching, kicking, or shooting bullets at each other. The reason for this wide application of the term is that further research began to indicate that Schjelderup-Ebbe had discovered much more than the secret of a hen's private life. In fact, the dominance hierarchy, of which the chicken-yard pecking order is an elementary example, has since been shown to be the basic form of social organization in all vertebrate species.

Among chickens, dominance relationships develop very easily. If two strange hens are put together in a small coop, bouts of pecking and flapping, accompanied by a great deal of squawking, will begin as soon as they find themselves competing for food and will continue until one of the two is finally driven off. In subsequent conflicts, the bird which lost the first fight will normally retaliate with less and less confidence until finally the winner need only threaten it to drive it out of the way. The two birds will now be able to co-exist with only a token show of friction. For poultry farmers, this means that the hens have settled down and will now be able to eat more food and lay more eggs. For social scientists, it means that a habitual contract has been established which will from now on allow two separate, individual animals to co-operate efficiently.

Of course, a hen coop is a highly artificial environment for the study of an animal society. The population is almost exclusively female and the birds are confined in an unnaturally small area. Under natural conditions, their food would be spread out over the countryside and they would spend nearly all their waking day in finding it. This makes it difficult to determine just how much of the chicken-run pecking order was natural to the original species and how much is the product of domestication and confinement.

In the early 1930s, the Austrian ethologist Konrad Lorenz settled a semi-wild jackdaw colony around his home at Altenberg. This gave him an excellent opportunity to study a completely undomesticated but social species in a region which could be described as typical, if not ideal, for jackdaws. Although jackdaw dominance is a long way from human dominance, the jackdaw version of the dominance hierarchy produced a number of surprisingly subtle and sophisticated features.

As soon as they were old enough, the young jackdaw males began to hammer out the pecking order among themselves much as Lorenz's knowledge of domestic animals had led him to expect. The social hierarchy they set up proved at least as rigid as that of domestic fowls. In fact, it appeared more perfectly linear and permitted fewer exceptions to the rule. On the other hand, several novel features attracted Lorenz's expert eye. By hen coop standards of social behaviour, it seems to be normal practice to peck everyone you have a right to peck as often as you like; but in the jackdaw world, there appears to be a sense of *noblesse oblige*. After the birds have established their positions, only the lower ranking individuals continue to bicker with one another. The higher-ups behave in an orderly way and treat their inferiors with aristocratic indifference. Even in the lower ranks, quarrels are normally conducted only between close neighbours on the pecking order ladder. Number five or number six in the hierarchy might bully number seven or number eight, but to pick on number twelve, it appears, would be regarded as improper.

Dominant chickens and jackdaw tyrants may seem very distant relatives of the dominant man. However, the pioneering efforts of Schjelderup-Ebbe and Lorenz have permanently altered our traditional idea of dominance. Far from being a magic quality with which only a few special individuals are born, it now appears to be a principle which applies throughout a whole community of animals and whose principal function is to provide leadership and internal order.

Monkey and Ape Societies

Once the pecking order had been discovered as the basic model of social organization among vertebrates, the ethologists proceeded to map out the ways that different animal species have adapted the system to suit their special needs. In particular, they wanted to examine those versions of the dominance system that characterize man's closest animal relatives.

Man is classified zoologically as a member of the primate order. He shares this status with four other species of ape and nearly two hundred species of monkey. Physiologically speaking, the apes are more closely related to man than are the monkeys, and the chimpanzee is usually considered the most manlike of all the apes due to his versatility and his relative lack of specialization. Since the time of Darwin, zoologists have been eager to point out that most of the qualities which appear to distinguish man from the rest of the animal world have, in fact, been developed to some extent by other primates. Far from being the unique creature he earlier believed himself to be, man has come to see himself as one species within the primate group – a species which has developed several valuable but typically primate characteristics to their fullest extent so far. Man represents that branch of the ape line which ventured out of the forests several million years ago to become a hunter on the open savannahs. The hunting life brought these adventurous ground apes into competition with highly specialized predators such as the large cats. This was evidently a major factor leading man's ancestors to push ahead with those primate characteristics we now regard as uniquely human.

As we might have expected, monkeys and apes have the most complex of all vertebrate societies. They force us to take a step away from the neatly stylized rank order we find in jackdaws. In the gorilla and the baboon, the dominance structure often inclines towards a tyranny of one undisputed leader. The power of this dictator can be so immense that it becomes difficult for an observer to identify number two and number three in the hierarchy below him. Central American howler monkeys represent the opposite extreme. Here the rank order has lost nearly all its significance due to the species' unusually successful adaptation in other ways to suit an environment of fruit-laden, tropical treetops. In between these extremes, all ape and monkey societies achieve co-operation with the aid of some sort of dominance hierarchy. The authority structure in the average monkey troop is seldom as distinctly defined as it is in the jackdaw society. Occasionally the whole community will follow a lieutenant rather than the captain in its daily search for food. A clan subordinate may sometimes be seen to win a minor argument against one of his betters. However, for all this apparent laxity, the dominance system is just as effective. The observer may need to be more patient in allotting each animal his exact rank, but the numbering can always be done.

Since man belongs among the apes, this is where we would expect to find the society most like our own. However, although the apes are our closest living relatives, they have stuck to a comparatively easygoing life in the forests. This evolutionary course stands in marked contrast to the career of man and his ancestors. As a result of their forest-bound life, the apes had felt no pressure to develop the efficient, highly co-operative hunting bands which distinguish our ape-man line. If we dismiss the apes, then we are forced to look among the largest ground-living monkey species in our search for close neighbours in the sphere of social design. In the end, the prizes must go to those much maligned relatives, the African baboon and the Asian macaque monkeys.

The baboon and the macaques are unusually successful and widespread species that have etched out a way of life very similar to that of our early prehuman ancestors. Fossil discoveries and new dating techniques have led scientists to believe that our earliest hunting-ape ancestors stood about four feet tall, weighed up to sixty pounds, and had a brain no larger than that of the modern gorilla. This was the proto-man who first hunted the African savannah with a weapon in his hand, and in this competitive profession, he must have depended heavily on developing his co-operative skills. The chimpanzee and the gorilla may tell us a great deal about other aspects of our ancestors' probable mental development, but the baboon and the macaques can offer more valuable clues to the way in which these proto-human societies were organized. Roughly speaking, these species are to the monkey tribe what man and his ancestors are to the apes – each the opportunistic plainsmen of their respective primate categories. The baboon's social system has developed along lines similar to man's because every day he faces the same sort of problem that must have confronted our ancestors for millions of years. All primates were initially designed for living in trees, so both man and monkey have had to come to terms with what was originally a hostile environment. The efficient co-operative structures of the baboon and the macaque, like man's, are among the principal adaptations which secured their survival on the ground.

A free-ranging troop of baboons or macaques will often be ruled by a single highly dominant male. (A baboon overlord may weigh as much as a hundred pounds and may live for as long as twenty-five years under natural conditions.) Alternatively, two or more adult males may form a ruling coalition by helping one another in disputes with anyone outside the alliance. Whatever arrangement exists at the top, a fairly clear-cut order of rank results, and all members of the troop are careful to show their superiors an appropriate degree of deference. The monkey's way of showing respectful submission consists of presenting his posterior. This resembles the human custom of bowing but it is done the opposite way around, with the anogenital region turned towards the dominant animal in imitation of the female's invitation to copulate. Although occasionally the dominant animals will mount the subordinate ones and pump the pelvic region a few times, as if copulating, they are evidently inhibited from biting a subordinate who humbles himself in this way – regardless of whether the subordinate is male or female. Juveniles and sub-adults make use of this inhibition whenever they find themselves uncomfortably close to a superior animal. By noting which animals present to which, observers can work out their relative rank order positions.

A specialized type of social behaviour in these monkey

societies, with which every regular zoo-goer will be familiar, takes the form of one individual's carefully picking through another's fur. This peaceful grooming of fellow troop members may seem the very opposite of dominance behaviour; but in fact the two are intimately related. To some extent this friendly grooming is concerned with cleaning and deticking. However, its most important function is undoubtedly social – the maintenance of stable dominance relationships between individual animals. This conclusion is indicated by the unequal laws of monkey grooming. Dominant males receive by far the most attention and they usually give the least. Female monkeys, who are normally subordinate to the males, are the most affiliative troop members and they do most of the grooming. Field workers who have invested many months in the intensive study of monkey habits point out that it is difficult to overestimate the importance of this friendly contact in keeping the peace and cohesion of primate societies. This view is supported by the fact that the ground-living baboons and macaques rank among the most authoritarian species of primate, and they also engage in more social grooming than any other monkey or ape, apparently as a counterbalance. A rigid rank order is obligatory in their odds-against environment, and these quiet spells of mutual grooming constantly reaffirm the troop's rank order relationships in a psychological atmosphere of affiliation and contentment.

Perhaps the most interesting aspect of the ground-living monkey's social behaviour concerns the sort of social responsibility that Konrad Lorenz discovered in his jackdaws. In the case of a baboon or a macaque, this could be called a code of honour or even morality. While the troop roams across the countryside in search of food, the most powerful males will normally be found in the middle of the procession keeping pace with the mothers and the very young. This is where their protection is most needed. (Sub-adult males range ahead of the troop, but they have to anticipate which way the top brass will want to go. If they make a mistake, they suddenly find themselves in the rear of the procession when they had thought they were out in front.) As with jackdaws, high-ranking males break up fights between their subordinates. In particular, if any other troop member threatens a mother or an infant, the dominant males immediately spring to the defence.

The full value of the baboon's morality can be appreciated when the troop is confronted by a serious threat, such as a leopard or an armed man. The dominant males stand firm in a semi-circle, facing the danger and protecting the troop, until the females and young have made their escape.

The Human Dominance Order

We can see immediately that elements of the baboon troop's dominance order system persist in human society. The most obvious example is the institutionalized rank order we find in the army. Every soldier wears a uniform to reduce his appearance to a common base and to indicate group solidarity. Badges and decorations are then added to signal measured differences in rank. A tight disciplinary system ensures that every individual keeps his proper place, and insubordination has frequently been treated as a capital crime. Here we have all the characteristics of an animal order developed to what is virtually an ideal form. The higher a soldier's rank, the more privileges he enjoys. Even the most modern army differs vastly in its authoritarian logic from the supposedly egalitarian society it serves. Traditionally, an army's spoils of conquest are doled out according to rank, and today officers continue to enjoy benefits their subordinates are denied.

Modern business corporations have borrowed their basic method of organization from the army. They involve themselves in take-overs. They launch drives to achieve their objectives. They often go to great lengths to encourage company loyalty among their employees. At the top of the business hierarchy, tycoons substitute for tyrants, and officers have become executives. Lower ranking salesmen are sent out into the field to manage and extend the company's territory. At all levels, the individual is surrounded by symbols of rank. The sort of desk he sits at, where and what he eats for lunch – all are governed by his position on the ladder. For many centuries, religious bureaucracies and secret societies have offered vivid examples of the human dominance order. Privilege, pay, occasionally immortality – all have been awarded according to the individual's hierarchical status.

These institutionalized dominance orders are easily interpreted as vestiges of the old way of life which have been deliberately retained for the sake of convenience. However, there is evidence to show that the hierarchy principle really runs much deeper than this and that it still plays a deceptively large part in man's everyday, informal relationships. Insolence, disrespect, looking up to others, being put in one's place – all these expressions reflect man's dominance-orientated social outlook. They have no meaning except within a hierarchical frame of reference, and yet they can be translated into any human language. They are used easily, almost thoughtlessly, millions of times a day in every possible social context.

Occasionally a lower ranking soldier may be insubordinate to his officers despite the threat of severe punishment. Servants occasionally behave insolently towards their masters. But a superior can never be insubordinate to an inferior no matter how hard he tries. A master cannot behave insolently in his treatment of a servant. A teacher cannot be cheeky to his pupils. These words identify the same dominance attitudes which a monkey expresses mostly with tactile and visual signals, and it is important to note that they all apply only to misdemeanours committed in an upward direction. If we want to identify improper behaviour directed downwards, we have to select from a completely different set of words. We may look down our noses at our inferiors. We may treat them condescendingly, haughtily, overbearingly, or high-handedly. Most people evidently find that the all-inclusive term 'misbehave' cannot communicate the rank order considerations which they often feel are essential to the description of improper behaviour.

All these terms are very ordinary parts of our everyday language. With hardly a moment's hesitation, the appropriate word is chosen millions of times a day to describe a fleeting and often subtle encounter between friends, business associates, strangers, foreigners, adults, juveniles, persons acting on behalf of a commercial organization, persons representing nobody but themselves, persons who have broken a minor law, persons standing righteously in their own backyards. Since so many of these words for improper behaviour have a strict, one-way limit on their usage, our ability to choose the correct word to suit any particular relationship in a fraction of a second proves the thoroughness with which modern men and women still arrange their social contacts on a hierarchical scale.

Frequent reference to dominance and subordination in our day-to-day language, as well as man's long-standing dependence on the division of large communities into caste hierarchies, clearly shows the extent to which the dominance order system continues to play a central part in human affairs. In fact, the anthropologist Lionel Tiger has referred to the dominance order as the universal spinal cord of a human community. Throughout history, certain basic social patterns along pecking order lines have recurred time and again with little variation. Human communities have displayed an overwhelming tendency to stay in the well-worn grooves of dominance and submission. Political revolutions break out with brilliant new social ideas. One or two of the new ideas may stay, but for the most part the hierarchy system reasserts itself in a new disguise and the egalitarian movement disintegrates.

The Will to Power

Man's mental picture of his own nature is undergoing a dramatic change. Until recently it was widely believed that at birth the human mind is a blank wax sheet on which all aspects of its eventual personality are then inscribed by personal experience and learning. Despite the impact made by Darwin nearly a century ago, the belief persisted that human nature must be infinitely adaptable. Now a series of breakthroughs in the biological and social sciences have made it clear that every human being inherits an extensive network of genetically determined dispositions. This basic instinctual pattern defines the potential behaviour of the fully developed adult. The extent to which man remains committed to the rules of the dominance order depends very largely on the exact nature of this genetically determined layout. In particular, the social scientist would like to know whether we construct formal and informal hierarchies in response to something we could call loosely a set of status instincts or whether these are nothing more than cultural inventions.

The idea of instinct was first used in connection with insects, whose lifelong behaviour patterns appear to be almost completely prescribed by a set of genetically inherited controls. No spider has to learn how to spin its intricate web. The ability to do this, the behavioural programme involved, is almost completely determined by the genetic design of the species. Today we know that this principle of instinctive behaviour applies to some extent throughout the animal world. But while the instinctive responses of an insect are relatively inflexible, the instinct controls we find in birds and mammals are frequently more pliable or open-ended. This means that the eventual form of the animal's behaviour can be modified to a greater extent by experience and learning.

The modern concept of modifiable instincts has led to a much clearer understanding of the inherited factors that channel man's cultural development and of the intricate relationship that exists between the hardware and the software of a human nervous system. In practice, it would probably be impossible to disentangle the instinctive component in an adult man's behaviour from the cultural component. The distinction remains useful only for the purposes of theoretical analysis. This means that a man can learn nothing that he does not have an inborn capacity to learn, while no inborn capacity can reveal itself without an appropriate environment. As a rule, we find that a type of behaviour which was important for the survival of our ancestors has become easy and pleasurable for us to learn but difficult to forget. Schoolmasters find little difficulty in teaching young boys physically violent competitive sports which mimic tribal fighting or dominance contests. It is much more difficult for them to foster an interest in abstract classwork.

Insects, birds, and mammals have all produced elaborate forms of social life. However, the extent to which these societies depend on a cultural pattern varies greatly. Ants and bees are often used as examples of creatures whose social system is wholly dictated by inherited chemistry. Bird societies are more adaptable, but in many cases their dependence on precisely tooled instincts remains astonishing. When we come to mammals, we find that the instinctive controls have lost still more of their detailed definition. Monkeys that have been brought up in total isolation and then released into the company of normally socialized adults find it impossible to maintain stable relationships. Without the opportunity to practise social patterns when they are young, the males never learn to copulate successfully and the females find it difficult to develop the normal maternal behaviour patterns. Man has developed the combination of modifiable instincts and cultural adaptation further than any other animal type. Nevertheless, an instinctive blueprint remains, and it is important to remember that these built-in patterns have evolved to suit not modern conditions but the substantially different way of life followed by man's ancestors over millions of years. The requirements for survival which have applied consistently to man's primate forefathers have evidently insured that a substantial part of his instinctive capacity for social interaction remains entirely devoted to fundamental types of dominance order behaviour.

One part of man's instinctive legacy in the dominance order sphere is apparent in the ease with which he is able to slip into dominant and subordinate social roles. This is evidently achieved by calling into action dominant and subordinate ego states — complex systems of mood, memory patterns, and habitual responses. As a rule, all social animals must remain subordinate to others for a large proportion of their lives. If they become dominant at all, this will usually occur only in later adulthood. For the individual to cope with these social requirements, he needs to be born with the capacity for both dominant and subordinate systems of behaviour.

The most widely acknowledged aspect of man's dominance order character is unquestionably his drive to climb the status ladder. People who have their need for dominance satisfied, who are generally looked up to by others, enjoy their social relationships more than those who are invariably looked down on. The desire for dominance has always been recognized as an important factor in man's social motivation. The belief that this is man's most fundamental urge was put forward by Arthur Schopenhauer, Friedrich Nietzsche, and later by Alfred Adler. Their views were necessarily limited to intelligent homespun theories, but the general principle that man inherits an adaptable drive towards social power is now being scientifically proved.

The question of who dominates whom occupies much of every other social animal's adolescence. Male readers will be able to test how applicable this rule is to human society by recalling their own teenage years. Generally speaking, the human male's adolescence consists of a series of high-voltage dominance contests which usually result in very small wins and losses on the status ladder. The American zoologist David

E. Davis recently analysed the biological motivation of adolescent street gangs. Not only is the street gang typically primate in its organization, he concluded, but the facts showed that fighting for social rank is at least partly instinctive.

We can get an idea of how important the dominance drive is from a study of those few human societies which have enjoyed over a long period of time a superabundance of all their normal economic requirements. In the past, these societies may have been rare. However, they raise the question of what happens to the normally dynamic social pattern under utopian circumstances. What do these societies do with their time once their principal needs have been cared for? We might have expected the result to be sexual debauchery and elaborate banqueting ceremonies; but in fact these have proved only minor ways of absorbing a rich society's superfluous time and effort. In all known cases, whether we are dealing with a relatively primitive tribe or the super-rich society of modern California, the most compelling way to spend the extra time and effort that wealth makes available has evidently been to construct a completely artificial status race.

Human society is traditionally thought of as the product of man's unique rationality. Perhaps he did not invent the social order, but he is led to believe that he depends on this rational faculty for understanding and obeying it. The discovery of surprisingly sophisticated social systems in apparently irrational animal types forces us to reconsider. Modern research has shown that we are linked to our remote primate ancestors by an unbroken continuum of co-operative social life. Far from being deliberately designed, we now know that human social structures have evolved through gradual amendments to the pattern that our scarcely rational simian ancestors developed millions of years ago. How has human society coped with our deeply ingrained commitment to the hierarchy system? To what extent does man remain a dominance order animal? To what extent do the age-old laws of hierarchical living continue to govern the growth of each unique human personality? In the process of answering these questions, we will need to look closely at some of the more glamorous aspects of human dominance that have until recently been regarded as beyond the scope of scientific investigation.

Most of the writing effort that has so far been expended on

examining man's dominance order inheritance has been spent on the relatively obvious fact that man is a born status-seeker. But this is probably not the most important clause in the legacy, and it is certainly not the most interesting. Why so many writers have limited themselves entirely to man's ladder-climbing ambition at the expense of other aspects of his dominance order character is difficult to divine. Whatever their reasons may have been, we are now going to go beyond this point.

CHAPTER 2

THE SUBMISSIVE PERSONALITY

We often imagine the typical subordinate as a rebellious or rancorous individual kept in his place by force – a potentially assertive character who longs to be dominant, or at least independent, but who cannot withstand the powers ranged against him. In fact, this somewhat mythical picture of the subordinate personality is far removed from the everyday reality. Historical evidence and clinical studies agree that the subordinate in a hierarchical structure often accepts his position willingly. Far from challenging his superior's rank, the submissive personality admires and looks up to his dominator. Most theoretical inquiries into human dominance have concerned themselves with the genetically programmed drive we feel as social animals to achieve status in our hierarchy. The psychological causes of human servility are usually overlooked. In man, as in other hierarchical species, this remarkable willingness to defer to rank order superiors is a predictable result of millions of years spent in a dominance order context.

We might have expected that the hierarchy formed by a band of free-ranging animals would continually adjust itself to day-by-day changes in confidence. However, when Konrad Lorenz studied his colony of jackdaws, he was struck by its peacefulness and social stability. What Lorenz has to say about his jackdaw community can be applied to all the free-living bird and mammal hierarchies that have so far been studied. Although play-fighting is characteristic of young animals in all social species, contests over rank are surprisingly rare among adults. Controlled experiments with domestic fowls, the observation of wolf packs, and field studies of baboon troops all confirm the stable nature of the dominance structure once it has been established. At one time, it was widely believed that all animal societies were characterized by continual and fierce status conflict. However, this conclusion was based on experience with domestic animals and the handful of undomesticated societies which could be studied only in zoo conditions. More recent research has shown that the bedlam of status rivalry which often ends in zoo animals killing each other is a result of the unnatural pressures of captivity. The chronic disorder of these caged communities indicates that something has gone drastically wrong with the sociable disposition of the inmates. Apparently the capacity for social interaction has been delicately tuned to suit the particular way of life that each species would lead in the wild.

In the last fifteen years, an enormous body of field research has shown that wild primates in particular accept subordinate status with astonishing docility. In fact, these studies of free-living primate communities give the clear impression that one of the major causes of dominance fighting, when it does break out, is a weak and loosely defined authority structure – a greater than usual degree of status uncertainty. Societies where the order of rank is more clearly defined are correspondingly free from social unrest. It would appear that one reason for the conservatism of these wild societies and the rarity of serious fights is that every individual quickly learns to avoid a clash with its proven superiors. The lower ranks are prepared to accept their places as long as their bosses make the position clear to them.

If we imagine the evolutionary history of social animals, we will see several good reasons for this conservative element in every dominance order structure. All the established hierarchical species we find today must have felt a continuous pressure over millions of years to compete for rank and consolidate their hierarchies as early as possible in the lives of their adolescent members. Any community that was a little too slow in sorting itself out would be unable to compete in the long run with its more disciplined neighbours. The better ordered societies would always be better prepared for the unexpected. They would always be better equipped to cope with the everyday difficulties of staying alive and reproducing in a more efficient and orderly way.

In the vast majority of vertebrate hierarchies, the male animals choose their mates in the order of their social rank. The number one in the pecking order takes first choice, the number two gets second choice, and so on down the line. This often means that the important business of mating must wait until the young males of each generation have settled their rank order disputes. As a result, a high premium is placed on making an early and stable settlement.

The more stable the hierarchy, the more secure each individual feels within it and the less distraction there will be from friendly co-operative effort. If every subordinate remained permanently on the alert to oust his superior at the first opportunity, and if every superior had to remain constantly on guard against these surprise attacks, then obviously the community would run the risk of disintegrating altogether. It would stand little chance in the inter-society competition. In the slow course of evolution, the successful societies that survived the competition have consistently been those that came to establish each new generation's dominance order most simply and quickly, and for whom, once a hierarchy had been decided, conservatism became all-important. We can draw a comparison here between the stability of the rank order in the wild and the concept of discipline in a human army. Every soldier's blind obedience to his rank order superiors is considered essential to the efficiency of a military unit – the one principle for which even individual initiative is thought to be worth sacrificing.

This emphasis on a swiftly established and lasting dominance order has had an important effect on the individual. For him it means the swift acceptance of a successful rival as an established superior. To construct a hierarchy, every individual status-seeker will have to switch off his desire to compete with those who have proved more than his match. If selective pressures called for the rapid and complete establishment of order in the community, then they also called for an equally quick and complete self-subordinating mechanism in the social animal's evolving psychology. The result of many millions of years' development in a social direction is that every hierarchical animal now possesses the ability to abandon his competitive feelings in the presence of an acknowledged superior – a special arrangement of psychological equipment which allows a weaker animal to accept the domination of a worthy leader.

Experiments with domestic fowls have given us an idea of how effective this submissive disposition can be in a social species with a relatively simple psychological makeup. By injecting a male sex hormone into low-ranking hens, they can be made more self-assertive. If they are then cooped up together with complete strangers, they will exert an abnormal degree of aggression. However, the same degree of hormone treatment will almost never result in the adjustment of an established rank order. In one experiment, a hen is given a pellet of the male hormone testosterone and is then placed in a pen full of untreated hens whom she has never met before. Immediately she begins to assert herself and chases all her fellow inmates around the enclosure. But as soon as she is returned to her own flock, she automatically resumes her normal social rank and makes no attempt to challenge any of her old superiors. Clearly the psychological power of habitual deference is a force to be reckoned with in bringing peace and stability to a society of chickens.

Similiar behaviour will often be seen in domestic dogs whenever a young puppy grows up under the domination of an older dog and continues to defer to him long after he has grown physically stronger. Studies carried out on chimpanzees and baboons in the wild have shown that an organized band of either species will sometimes be led by an ageing male who is thoroughly respected by all other adults although he is now clearly weaker than many of them. If he is threatened at all, it will only be by juvenile males who are too young to have known him in his heyday.

As each young animal establishes his position in the authority structure, the losers in every community learn to play subordinate roles in their dealings with one-time opponents. Every animal will gain steadily in overall seniority as the members of older generations weaken and die and as youngsters gradually swell the total number of subordinates beneath him. But within his own generation, every individual will normally keep much the same position that he established for himself in his youth. Eventually, all the individual capitulations each animal is forced to perform add up to an effective abandonment of his status-climbing aspirations as a whole and to total acceptance of a greater or smaller body of acknowledged superiors. In a closed community, every familiar face the individual comes into contact with will now be recognized as a proven superior or as a junior whose status claims he can afford to discount.

Experiments in Human Deference

The psychological capacity for social deference is highly developed in non-human primates. This may be the main reason why rank order disputes among the larger apes are so rare. However, what the psychologist would like to know is the exact extent to which man makes use of a similar psychological disposition in constructing human society. To what extent does the corresponding behaviour in a subordinate human being indicate a similar psychological structure?

Between 1960 and 1965, psychologists at Yale University conducted a now famous series of experiments to test the psychological mechanism of obedience in a typical cross-section of Americans. Working on the assumption that obedience is a basic element in the structure of social life and that 'the very life of society is predicated on its existence', they tested the response of subjects to the domination of a specially trained authority figure. The part was played by a thirty-one-year-old high school biology teacher who was instructed to be firm and impassive throughout the experiment. In addition, the experiment required a victim, played by a forty-seven-year-old accountant, who was also trained for his special role. Observers found him mild-mannered and likeable. The technique involved a fake experiment within the real experiment, designed to keep the subjects ignorant of the real purpose of the test. From the subjects' point of view, the experimental procedure was essentially quite simple. They were told they were going to help perform an experiment to test the effect of punishment on learning.

At the start of the experiment, the victim or 'learner' was strapped into an electric chair apparatus in an adjoining room, One at a time each subject was then placed in front of what appeared to be an electric shock generator, carefully made to look like the real thing, and he was given a sample shock of forty-five volts to prove that the apparatus was genuine. Switches on the dummy generator were labelled with voltages that ranged from 15 to 450 volts. They were also labelled in groups under the headings Slight Shock, Moderate Shock, Strong Shock, Very Strong Shock, Intense Shock, Extreme Intensity Shock, Danger: Severe Shock. The two final shock intensities were marked XXX. Subjects were instructed to shock the learner and to raise the degree of shock one level every time the learner flashed a wrong answer to a series of ten words which he was supposed to memorize correctly. Since the learner had been briefed never to give all the correct answers, the subjects were obliged to give increasingly severe shocks if they were to follow the instructions they had been given. The idea was to see how severely subjects 'under orders' were prepared to hurt the victim, who was instructed to bang on the walls when the generator registered 300 volts.

The subjects who refused to continue with the experiment at any stage were termed 'defiant', while those who went all the way were labelled 'obedient'. Fourteen senior Yale psychology students were asked to guess how many of the subjects would go on to administer the most severe shocks. They estimated that few, if any, would go beyond the fourth of the nine shocks graduations – Very Strong Shock. In fact, all their estimates proved way off the mark. Of the forty subjects tested, all went beyond this point. Five dropped out at Intense Shock and eight at Extreme Intensity Shock. But, significantly, twenty-six went beyond Danger: Severe Shock, all the way to the last calibration marked XXX.

Interviews with subjects after the test left no doubt that they believed they were causing another human being extreme pain. It was also clear that most of them were emotionally upset by the experience. During the experiment, especially when they were administering the most severe shocks, subjects were observed to sweat, tremble, stutter, bite their lips, groan, and dig their fingernails into their flesh. Fourteen of the forty subjects showed nervous smiling and laughter, which the observers noted seemed out of place, even bizarre. Three suffered uncontrollable seizures, and in general the tension reached extremes that are seldom found in scientific laboratories. The most remarkable point to keep in mind is that all the subjects were free to defy the experimenter and end the experiment at any point. Obedience could only be induced by verbal prods from the experimenter. These increased in severity from 'Please continue' or 'Please go on' to 'You have no other choice, you *must* go on.' The experimenter, dressed in a technician's grey coat and obviously regarded by the subjects as an authority figure, was instructed to be firm but polite at all times. As long as he remained unmoved, the subjects of the experiment were clearly prepared to accept his definition of the situation and to abandon their independent judgment of how much pain they were morally justified in inflicting.

In the opinion of the psychologists conducting the test, the fact that 65 per cent of all the subjects could be pushed to go through with it proved the great strength of man's tendency to obey authority. All the subjects had been taught from childhood that hurting another person is a fundamental breach of moral conduct. Yet a clear majority of perfectly normal people abandoned this principle in following the instructions of an authority who had no special powers to enforce his commands. In subsequent experiments, victims were instructed to cry out in pain, to complain of heart trouble, and to plead to be set free. But subjects continued to shock them on command. With what Stanley Milgram, the head of the research team, describes as 'numbing regularity', people were induced by their respect for authority to inflict on others what seemed to be extreme pain and the possibility of permanent injury.

Army instructors, who have all the power of the state behind them to enforce their commands, reduce the obedience of those placed under them to a conditioned reflex with the aid of such techniques as parade ground drill. In this way, it appears, they are able to exploit the social animal's potential for submission to such an extent that insubordination is practically unheard of. The continuous show of deference in a modern army (saluting, standing to attention, extreme politeness of address, etc.) compares very closely with the submissive behaviour of subordinates in baboon troops and wolf packs. The degree to which military-style authoritarianism can bring about a complete withdrawal of defiance, even an eagerness to defer, is illustrated by Bruno Bettelheim's account of a year he spent as a prisoner in the notorious Nazi concentration camps of Dachau and Buchenwald in 1938–9. Bettelheim, a prominent psychologist, draws attention to a frequently overlooked function of these camps within the Nazi political system. The Gestapo used them primarily as experimental laboratories, to study ways of breaking civilian resistance and of forcing defiant personalities to defer to the authority of the Nazi regime. The psychological adjustment prisoners made after three years' exposure to extreme cruelty, starvation, and hardship indicated just how effective authoritarian measures can be in bringing not only complete submission to authority but total assimilation of its values.

Bettelheim noted that the first indication of his co-prisoners' acceptance of the Nazi guards' dominance was that they began to imitate the guards' vocabulary of curses and threats when expressing aggression towards each other. When seasoned prisoners were put in charge of their fellow inmates, they often behaved more cruelly than the Gestapo themselves. Prisoners who had been in camp for about three years identified with their warders to the extent of altering their clothes to look like Gestapo uniforms. They went to great lengths to lay their hands on real pieces of Gestapo uniforms and when asked why they did so, openly admitted that they liked to look like the guards. They went so far as to imitate the guards' off-duty pleasures. One of these was the game of beating each other to see who could stand the pain the longest. Seasoned prisoners began to believe that the Gestapo rules were desirable standards of human behaviour in the camp situation. This process extended to accepting Nazi values of race discrimination which had been alien to them before they were subjected to the persistent cruelties of the concentration camp.

The Art of Self-abandon

The experiments at Yale and in the Nazi concentration camps clearly illustrate the capitulation of the human personality to authoritarian pressures. The same capacity for self-subordination reveals itself in many other situations. Observation of front-line troops in World War II showed that soldiers who had spent long periods under intense emotional strain began to idealize and overestimate the power of their officers. Under the stress of battle, the adult relationship between soldier and officer becomes blurred by a transfer of childlike love, hate, and dependency feelings onto the person in authority. In addition to idealizing his officer, who appears to control his destiny, the soldier – the individual under authority – is strongly motivated to follow all instructions uncritically in an attempt to maintain the approval and support of his superior.

This hero worship of authority figures closely resembles the feelings of many patients in psychoanalysis towards their doctor. Still another parallel can be found in the way people behave when they become involved in an angry or excited mob. The individual caught up in an inflamed mob loses all self-consciousness and respect for conventional values – uncritically adopting the values of the mob in their place. Early theorists compared this return to a childlike, emotionally dependent state with what happens to a subject slipping into a hypnotic trance.

The classic psychoanalytic explanation of the dramatic change in behaviour of the Gestapo camp victims is that the treatment dealt out to them caused them to regress to a state of childlike dependence on their guards; they came to regard their captors as father figures. There is an obvious similarity in the childlike attitude of these concentration camp victims towards their guards, the childlike attitude of battle-weary soldiers towards their leaders, the way in which a patient undergoing psychoanalysis begins to treat his doctor as a father figure, the attitude of the hysterical mob towards the demagogue at the microphone, and the extreme dependence of the hypnotized subject. Psychologists who have made a special study of hypnosis emphasize that a hypnotist's success depends on his prestige in the eyes of his subject and on the subject's own submissiveness and lack of criticism. Sigmund Freud maintained that the hypnotist triggers an innate self-subordinating mechanism in the subject's mind, a mechanism which is first activated by the child's need to subordinate himself to his parents, and especially to his father.

In 1921, when Freud tried to explain the biological origin of this self-subordinating disposition, there were few studies available of non-human social behaviour. Nevertheless, his intuition brought him close to the conclusions these studies now indicate. It appeared to Freud that the basic human group consists of a masterful leader and a band of more or less equal subordinates. Freud agreed with earlier theorists that crowds generally have a passion for authority, a thirst for obedience. However, he maintained that the extent of this thirst depended on the individual members' feelings of self-centredness and self-assurance. To use the psychological language Freud developed, individuals with strong and independent egos have no need to place themselves under an idealized leader. On the other hand, individuals who have little self-confidence or who have for some special reason lost faith in their ability to run their own lives are more strongly driven to fall into a childlike state of dependence and are eager to exchange self-control for control by an outside authority. Their instinctive ability to defer to a leader develops a hair trigger. They fall into a state of mind which makes them yearn for a powerful ally to whom they can hand over all their responsibilities.

The increasingly widespread science of political brainwashing illustrates how easily man's servile tendency can be exploited once the practical applications of dominance theory have been recognized. Brainwashing techniques developed in the last few decades by various political police forces throughout the world are in all cases aimed at conditioning a prisoner's emotional state until he voluntarily switches off his defiance to the interrogator's demands and accepts them as his own. A step short of hypnosis, the brainwashing process invariably begins by placing the victim in solitary confinement for long periods of time. This is sometimes combined with forcing him to perform humiliating tasks and it aims at reducing his self-esteem, thus sapping his determination to resist. He is then subjected to periods of interrogation which may go on continuously for several days. During all this time, the use of strong lights, noise, bullying treatment, and stimulants like amphetamine keep him at the highest possible nervous pitch. As soon as he shows signs of cracking, he is allowed to relax. At this point, he is sometimes treated in a kindly way. Significantly, this is when the victim is most likely to switch his allegiance from his own system of values to that of his interrogators. The constant psychological pressure of domination appears to build up in him a longing to submit, to escape the emotional insecurity of resistance. His interrogator's sudden transformation into a nice guy gives him just the moral excuse that he needs. A parasitic super-ego takes the place of his own, he confesses that he was in the wrong, and the brainwashing process is complete.

Something very similar to the social animal's submissive response can be detected in the psychology of human crowds. We find the same process operating, in what is probably closer to its original context, in the behaviour of soldiers under stress. It crops up again in religious indoctrination. A major component of hypnotism and the self-subordinating element in religious faith both appear to be extreme permutations of a psychological device that evolved in social vertebrates as an interpersonal link mechanism. The professional psychoanalyst may encounter another exaggerated expression of this device in a patient's transference to his therapist. However, these extreme examples need not blind us to the normal form of a social animal's submission operating in our everyday social life. Viewed in its ordinary, day-to-day proportions, the submissive attitude need not entail the full hypnotic fascination a demagogue holds for a frenzied crowd. In the normal coming and going of a human community, the effects are less spectacular, but the psychological process remains essentially the same.

The spontaneous formation of grooming-clusters around baboon troop leaders and the subordinate wolf's adoration for his pack leader are both good examples of the fascination that accompanies the subordinate attitude in non-human social relationships. Whether or not the extreme systems of fascination and imitation are normally present in man, as they were among the victims of Dachau and Buchenwald, the process of self-subordination is always accompanied by a certain paralysis of the individual's self-centred thoughts and motives. Even in the most mundane of human relationships, the individual who accepts a dependent status develops a barrier of inhibitions that prevents him from relying on his own judgment and initiative in the company of a superior. His perception of the superior is distorted. The greater the dominance gap, the more complete will be the subordinate's psychological capitulation. This is borne out by the extraordinary fascination famous personalities hold for the ordinary people with whom they come into casual contact.

The exact way in which a subordinate submits to authority will obviously vary from one social species to another. The various psychological and physiological processes that contribute to the deferential behaviour of a human being will presumably be more amenable than most to cultural conditioning. Nevertheless, the presence of an underlying genetic foundation is beyond question. Although we may feel that this primitive pattern of psychological processes is no longer necessary and that rational human society should be able to get along without it, we cannot escape the fact that it continues to operate all around us.

Dominant and Subordinate Personalities

The process of emotional subordination performs the key function of making one animal follow another. It must rank as one of the most important elements in the sociable disposition of several hundred vertebrate species. In particular, it still plays an important part in the working of our own society, and, as Freud anticipated fifty years ago, this individual suspension of assertive attitudes results in two kinds of psychologies. The first of these is to be found in the man who habitually defers to nearly everyone he meets and whose ego-ideal is in this way transferred to other persons or personalized institutions. Such a man is emotionally dependent on these authority figures to the same degree that he is obedient to them. At the opposite extreme, we encounter Freud's primal leader – the awesome figure who loves no one but himself and whose narcissism is tempered only by practicality. A characteristic of this personality type is that he feels little or no need of others. He is self-confident and self-sufficient. He defers to no one and enjoys a high level of self-esteem because his ego and his ego-ideal are one. To say that his ego and his ego-ideal coincide is to say that this high-power personality is exactly what he wants to be. Unlike most people, he feels little or no motivation towards self-improvement or the improvement of his image in other people's eyes.

We must remember that Freud was contrasting two theoretical extremes. In practice, we would expect to find every gradient between them. Nevertheless, clinical studies support Freud's theorizing more strongly than we might have guessed, and they show that in practice people are acutely aware of their positions on the dominance–subordination scale. They indicate that a human community can be divided up into generally dominant or generally dependent personality types, not so obviously in accordance with how they behave but in accordance with how they feel about themselves and each other. The classic experiment along these lines was conducted in the late 1930s by the American psychologist Abraham Maslow, the pioneer of scientific research into human dominance behaviour.

Maslow was able to demonstrate that some individuals in the general population feel dominant over practically all the people they meet while others almost always feel subordinate.

He began his experiments by subjecting a large number of men and women to a carefully controlled analysis that included extensive interviews, hypnosis, dream interpretations, questionnaire studies, observations of each subject's behaviour, and the subject's own reports on his behaviour. On the basis of this analysis, he was able to conclude that people can be divided into high-dominance, low-dominance, and middle-dominance types. Each of these personality types was found to behave in a complex but characteristic way in all the affairs of their daily life. Maslow's experiments showed that it was surprisingly easy to place people in the correct dominance category simply by asking them to describe the way they felt about themselves.

The high-dominance person describes himself as feeling a strong sense of self-respect. He feels masterful and superior to others in a very general sense. He feels sure of his ability to handle other people and to succeed in anything he sets his mind to. He never feels shy, timid, or embarrassed. At the other end of the scale, the low-dominance person describes himself as feeling inferior to most people. He doubts his ability ever to manage them. He does not think highly of himself. He would rather be like somebody else if he were given the chance.

Maslow emphasizes that high-dominance feeling should not be confused with domineeringness. The high-dominance personality is not necessarily a nasty person. High-dominance feeling implies self-confidence rather than aggressiveness. Instead of low-dominance feeling, we could substitute a lack of self-confidence, a feeling of unworthiness or low ego level. Maslow adds the interesting comment that every individual's feeling of dominance may fluctuate, but only within a small range of the total possible scale. Any one person is aware of only his own range of dominance feelings and tends to think that this range is very wide. In fact, compared with the total range of dominance feelings in the general population any individual's range of variation in dominance outlook is usually fairly small.

For twenty million years at least, and probably for quite a lot longer, man and his primate ancestors have been social animals. The human line has spent a long time evolving in a social direction, and evidence of the sort we have reviewed here indicates that man inherits certain special psychological qualities and capacities that are characteristic of any long-standing hierarchical species. We may like to assume at this point that modern man is successfully replacing the pecking order element in his cultural system with a preferable egalitarian foundation. However, it is not in his power at the moment to push back the genetic clock. At this stage, there are three specific character traits of human society which it clearly shares with other animal societies and which deserve to be singled out for special mention.

In the first place, our social past has ensured that every individual of the species inherits a drive to climb the dominance ladder. All social vertebrates are status-seekers, and *Homo sapiens* is no exception to the rule. A community needs capable leadership and an efficient order of priority. Competition between communities has developed the sort of animal who will devote a large part of his available energy to winning a distinct and preferably a high-ranking social position. This has resulted in what classical theorists have called a 'will to power'. Whatever we call it, it is this psychological sensitivity to dominance which gives meaning to such words as 'fame', 'respect', 'glory'.

On the other hand, it follows that if a community is to cooperate efficiently then its status-minded members must eventually stop their competitive ladder climbing and accept the positions they have reached so far. This has resulted in a second distinctly hierarchical characteristic. Man, like every other successful social vertebrate, has evidently inherited a well-developed capacity for deference which checks his dominance ambitions at appropriate moments.

The third part of this social legacy is a logical result of such a capacity for subordination. Since everybody must settle for a unique interpersonal position relative to everybody else's, we are left with a society of unequals. Every individual involved in human society consistently operates within a fairly stable mood somewhere in between the two extremes of boisterous self-assertion and timid accommodation. This scale of dominance feelings should not be confused with the formal rank order within the community, but there is of course a connection between the two. The stability of a community obviously depends to some extent on a fairly close matching of each individual's ego level to his official rank. The difference in ego level between people at opposite ends of the scale is probably smaller today than it has often been in the past. However, no one can reasonably doubt that considerable differences still exist. For the sake of clarity, much of what follows will involve contrasting the two extreme psychological types at the very top and the very bottom of the ladder. At the same time, we should not lose sight of the various shades of dominance feeling that exist between them.

CHAPTER 3

CONFRONTATION BEHAVIOUR

The capacity to think and feel in a subordinate pattern must rank as one of the most important psychological adaptations which the individual had to undergo in order to bring about a dominance order way of life. It could never have been easy for a defeated animal to suddenly forget his competitive feelings and switch to regular deference towards his victorious opponent. The development of special emotional techniques of submission made it possible for the loser of a status contest to accept the domination of his victor on amicable terms although this meant taking second place to him in almost every way. At the same time, it would be a mistake to think that this remarkable capacity for accepting leadership completes the list of ways in which man's brain has evolved to suit life in a hierarchical community.

We have no way of knowing the full extent to which a defeated animal resents the bites and bruises inflicted on him during a battle with a fellow pack member, and we may not be justified in reading into the situation anything like the shame and humiliation which would trouble a sensitive human ego under similar circumstances. But from the point of view of conserving lives in the wild, where even a scratch may lead to infection and a damaged limb probably means death, the less actual fighting there is in a dominance contest, the better it will be for all concerned. Serious fighting over dominance positions would inevitably result in serious injuries to healthy young status-seekers and make dominance contests expensive affairs from the community's point of view. After being carried by the community as dependent youngsters, growing males would be incapacitated just at the time when they were about to shoulder adult responsibilities. For the great majority of hierarchical species, injurious dominance fights have proved a consistent handicap in the contest for survival between communities. As a result, most present-day examples of vertebrate society have found more or less effective ways of getting around the problem. In most cases, serious fighting within the community has been greatly reduced by the introduction of relatively harmless forms of dominance competition. In addition to the evolution of special submissive equipment, the original form of the dominance fight has been ritualized and a pseudo-fight has evolved.

The confrontation ritual performed by two male fallow deer provides an illustration of how pseudo-fighting operates in many mammal species. First, the two handsome opponents engage in a broadside display during which they show off their bodily hulk and hence their probable strength to the best advantage. For several minutes they goose-step beside each other and wave their enormous antlers up and down. Finally, they swing their antlers together with a crash and settle down to an exhausting but seldom harmful pushing match that will eventually decide which animal is to take priority.

Ritualized contests of this type are not confined to hierarchical species. An almost ceremonial contest can often be observed among animals we could not normally call social. Frequently such a ritual is used to decide who stays on and who leaves a particular hunting territory or breeding ground. In all these cases, however, we could say that a comparatively harmless contest over temporary or local dominance has replaced a more serious kind of fight. Moreover, while many pseudo-fighting species may not be hierarchical, it remains true that most if not all hierarchical vertebrates are pseudo-fighters.

A superficial study of modern human society might leave an observer with the impression that man has rid himself of these confrontation rituals that were once an essential part of the dominance order system. But a closer look reveals that the primitive confrontation still plays an extremely important backstage role in our social life. Modern human adults frequently manage to avoid the full-blown pseudo-fight characteristic of other hierarchical species. However, we will find that this apparent ability to get around the problem often represents no more than a highly sophisticated ritualization of the primitive encounter.

The Logic of a Pseudo-fight

Some of the most closely studied laboratory pets in recent years have belonged to a small, predominantly tropical group of fish known as the cichlids. Among the many revelations to emerge from their period in the scientific limelight is a particularly instructive version of the ritualized pseudo-fight. Despite the fact that they are such distant relatives of *Homo sapiens*, cichlids give a clear picture of the patterns of behaviour which make up a pseudo-fight. Of added interest is the fact that different species within the cichlid group have developed the ritual to different degrees of sophistication. One result is that the ethologist can now compare the simple forms against the more elaborate ones to get some idea of how the process of ritualization evolved.

Like the fallow deer, the two contestants in a cichlid pseudo-fight will first engage in a broadside display. This movement appears to have arisen out of a conflict between two opposing emotions – the desire to attack angrily and the desire to flee. As the tension rises, they begin to direct currents of water at one another with strong tail-beating movements. In this way, each contestant is made aware of the other's approximate size and probable fighting power. (In some species of fish, the impression of size and strength conveyed during this period of display is enhanced by spectacular markings or greatly enlarged and colourful fins. Like the stag's antler's, these appear to have evolved as a consequence of the awe-inspiring effect they have in a confrontation.) The important feature of the cichlid's pseudo-fight is that the fish will almost never go so far as to injure each other. In some species, they may never even touch. They dart threateningly forward but stop short at the last moment. The war of nerves ends when one of the contestants turns tail and swims away. The evolutionary value of this competitive ritual lies in its ability to decide which of two animals is stronger without causing serious damage to the weaker one. The resulting behaviour appears sporting to the human observer because a very similar principle underlies all human sport, possibly for reasons more closely associated to the instinctive behaviour of cichlids and fallow deer than we usually imagine.

Closer to home, we find confrontations enacted with similar formality by domestic cats. Cats are considered to be only semisocial animals. Nevertheless, here again we find that once two animals have decided their respective dominance standing, subsequent disputes will usually be settled on the basis of display rather than physical fighting.

The most familiar example of a confrontation ritual in the animal world is probably the pseudo-fight in which two strange dogs engage. In this case, the contestants pace stiff-legged towards each other with their heads high and their tails erect. The closer they get to each other, the more tense they become and the more slowly they advance. For a moment it looks as though they are going to pass each other, but then they stop broadside on and express their confidence by sniffing inquisitively at each other's rear end. This is the crisis of the canine confrontation, and a dog whose nerve breaks at this point will curl his tail defensively between his legs and wheel away from his rival. A pair of more evenly matched dogs will remain in this stiff pose for some minutes. Then, as the tension rises, they begin to growl, wrinkling their noses, and expose their fangs. Unless one of the animals gives in fairly promptly, a serious fight is now liable to break out. However, the challenge is almost never maintained up to this critical point. More often, the eventual loser quickly shows by the anxious way he looks about him that he is more concerned with getting out of the predicament than he is with getting acquainted.

As in the confrontation behaviour of almost every other vertebrate species, this elaborate performance gives the two opponents an opportunity to size each other up before making a serious commitment. The longer and more gradual the escalation into a fight, the better for all concerned. In the first place, these elaborate procedures absorb the energy that would otherwise have been spent on injurious fighting. In the second place, they create an artificial contest in which the probable loser can back down before he gets hurt. The remote ancestors of these modern contestants presumably lacked such sophisticated methods of show-fighting. But since their day, the forces of natural selection have evidently favoured a type of animal who came to string out his declaration of challenge into an ever more elaborate performance and who was capable of anticipating his imminent defeat before suffering any serious damage. For convenience, we speak of the evolutionary value of this elaborated approach to dominance contests. However, we have to remember that this is always a result of natural selection, and the idea of purpose is used here only as an analogy. The individual winners of status contests enjoy a gain in dominance, and, wherever this affects the process of sexual selection, their winning characteristics will tend to be exaggerated in future generations. At the intercommunity level of selection, these developments in the confrontation procedure would have found favour, for example, because they minimized injury to up-and-coming youngsters.

This new accent on the display of aggressive signals rather than the actual performance of aggression has now come to apply so widely that it would be wrong to say that contests for dominance order position are normally decided in a fight. For the student of social evolution, the awe-inspiring ornaments of a rutting stag and the colourful dances of Siamese fighting fish mark a significant development in social finesse. They indicate that for these present-day animals the confrontation procedure that was originally limited to the business of squaring off for action and just a short preamble to the real contest has itself become the arena of dominance decisions.

The mention of social finesse brings us back to the subject of primate behaviour. The social habits of the monkeys and apes involve an unprecedented degree of individual variation and learning. Nevertheless, the typical confrontation display of an aggressive primate has developed into a similarly stylized sequence of gestures, each containing an increasing degree of threat. Occasionally these may lead into a serious fight, but normally a peaceful solution will be reached long before the preparatory ritual has been completed.

The gorilla provides us with a good example of how this process works in man's nearest relatives. Despite his ferocious appearance and his frequent use as a monster by Hollywood film-makers, the gorilla is in reality a skilful pseudo-fighter. Young males who get out of line are 'eldered' rather than attacked. When confronted by a human in circumstances that prevent escape, a gorilla will run through the threat motions of glaring fiercely, beating his chest, then eventually charging. These patterns of behaviour reflect progressive degrees of anger, and from all accounts a fully grown male can put on a frightening show. However, the charge is almost never pressed home. It is considered a great disgrace among the local Africans to be bitten by a gorilla: it proves that the victim panicked and ran away. Careful observation of confrontations between gorillas in the wild has turned up some equally interesting facts. On those occasions when hostility has reached an extreme pitch, two animals may come to the point of charging each other fiercely. But instead of the frightful battle we would expect, each takes a hurried slap at the other, then both rush off into the jungle in opposite directions.

In general, the confrontation procedure of gorillas and chimpanzees reflects the predictable trend of primate behaviour towards subtlety and sophistication. In many instances, the question of dominance is decided with scarcely any ill-feeling or evident competition at all, so acutely can the probable loser of the contest read the necessary signals contained in his opponent's appearance and behaviour.

The British zoologist Michael Chance has made a careful analysis of the evolutionary importance of conflict avoidance in primates. He suggests that the highly developed intelligence of monkeys and apes evolved partly in answer to the subordinate primate's more than ordinary need to side-step confrontations skilfully. No other mammal is subjected to anything like the persistent threats and conflicts which plague a subordinate baboon or macaque monkey. Not the least of the causes of friction in monkey troops is the almost constant sexual receptivity of at least one female in the troop at any given time. Experiments have shown that the primate's subtle ability to avoid domestic conflict is dependent on the part of the brain we call the neocortex. The neocortex is generally accepted as the seat of human intelligence and rationality. Michael Chance puts forward the theory that the exceptional development of the neocortex in primates was largely the result of the fact that young males had to learn to control their emotional impulses in the face of constant sexual and social provocation. He adds that this development of the primate brain in the cause of social harmony may have been the critical factor which pre-adapted man's ancestors to their intensively co-operative hunting life on the plains, as well as to the subsequent evolution of skills in such spheres as tool using and language.

Man's skill in dealing with the dominance issue may or may not have had so extensive an influence on his whole evolutionary course. The important point is that most human beings are at least as sensitive to the elements involved in a human confrontation as are the stag and the gorilla to the warning signals that play an equivalent part in theirs. Among children and primitives, the pseudo-fight consists of threatening gestures such as shaking the fist and shouts of defiance such as 'Who do you think you are?' or 'Do you think I'm scared of you?' Urban man may appear to handle his daily conflicts more harmoniously, but the angry exhibitionist lies just under the surface, ready to appear whenever he is caught off guard. Anyone who has watched the behaviour of two motorists involved in a minor accident will have seen how easily a human confrontation can develop. Unless they are unusually controlled, both parties can be expected to shout angrily, to wave their arms about in the air, and to stare menacingly into each other's faces. The show they put on suggests they are about to break into a serious fight. But in practice, the effort involved in this aggressive display is usually sufficient to consume their anger, and the situation almost never escalates further.

In view of man's exceptional resourcefulness, it should come as no surprise to find that he has eliminated more of the problems implicit in the social ranking process than any of his animal relatives. In a human context, the confrontation procedure does more than simply inhibit the breaking of bones. Even the monkey appears sufficiently sensitive to his social position to feel humiliated when a superior bullies him, and he will often reassert his self-esteem by bullying a weaker colleague in return. The winning and losing of status contests in human society threatens to leave behind it a still greater residue of hurt pride. Accordingly, we find that the most subtle features of human confrontation behaviour are not so much concerned with saving lives as with saving the contestants a maximum of self-esteem. Far from allowing himself to become involved in a disastrous fight, man has learned how to avoid, in most situations, even the slighter humiliation of a lost confrontation. As a rule, he is able to see an approaching showdown so far in advance that it is rare for two adults to confront one another with any serious intention of going as far as a physical fight. Some computing device inside each would-be contestant predicts the outcome so quickly, and on the basis of so little information, that an interim solution has often been tacitly agreed on before the genial opponents have finished shaking hands.

One way in which we can reduce the humiliation involved in a dominance contest is to justify our capitulation with more or less fraudulent rationalizations. Cultural traditions make available a whole range of justifications to suit practically any situation. In addition, the fully socialized adult develops a considerable talent for imagining how a confrontation might occur in the future. He quickly learns to recognize the kind of situation that could develop into a confrontation and to take precautionary steps at a very early stage. When the possibility of a confrontation seems remote, he relaxes. He feels socially secure. He may even take small liberties in his conversation. When he senses a confrontation approaching, he begins to feel more anxious and begins to reconsider the possible misinterpretations that could be placed on what he is about to say. The adult human's well-ordered sensitivity to all the cues apparent in any social situation enables him to measure his distance from the confrontation in plausible, sequential steps. He imagines how one act could lead to another and bring him progressively closer to the crisis point. He knows that the nearer he gets to High Noon, the more humiliating will it be to withdraw. As soon as the likely loser realizes that his opponent is prepared to approach the full-blown showdown in longer, easier strides than he is, he backs down.

For the most part, modern man avoids the serious status fights and even the highly emotional confrontations of his animal cousins with the aid of his superlative talent for strategy and diplomacy. At first, the peaceful settlements we make with one another may seem to prove that we no longer operate on the same social wavelength as other animal groups. However, although many men in our society may never reach the fist-waving stage, they must have a well-founded dread of what a confrontation feels like in order to avoid it so neatly. Our ability to foresee a confrontation developing out of a future situation in fact reveals a greater rather than a lesser sensitivity to the emotionally stirring cues involved. In other words, the fear of a confrontation still plays an important undercover role in establishing and maintaining our social structure. The threatened physical contest behind most informal status conflicts is recognized from boyhood as the court of final appeal. Many fully adult men continue to feel honour-bound to accept the invitation to step outside even when they do not normally evaluate themselves on the basis of their fist-fighting ability. The primitive physical challenge becomes particularly difficult to ignore whenever women are involved as spectators. It no doubt takes years of personal self-assurance to discount physical violence entirely as a means of deciding rank order issues.

This sensitivity to the various cues involved in a confrontation presumably differs slightly from one individual to another. For one thing, each individual's picture of the confrontation is likely to be influenced by personal memories, such as the particular physical features and behaviour patterns of those opponents who thrashed him in childhood fist fights. On the other hand, certain common elements can be detected in the image of the confrontation, and this indicates that our species may have a typical confrontation sequence comparable to those we have been able to map out more precisely for other dominance order animals. The human being's sensitivity to his species-specific confrontation cues is likely to be more amenable to experience and learning than that of any other animal. Yet for the most part, the particular physical characteristics and behaviour signals that elicit confrontation behaviour in a middle-aged Anglo-American are much the same as those that arouse the Chinese schoolboy, the Indian peasant, or the primitive African tribesman.

Sensitivity to Body Size

In any community of wild animals, an important factor in deciding status contests is usually physical strength. Few social animals enjoy the psychological ability to gang up against a tyrant and in only a handful of primate societies are individual rank order positions affected to any great extent by cultural factors. Of course, the determination and confidence with which each animal puts his physical strength to use are also important. However, muscular power and confidence cannot be entirely divorced. Now that so many social animals have learned to decide their relative rank on the basis of a confrontation ritual rather than on an actual fight, displays of confidence have become more important, and less emphasis is placed on the strength and skill that were needed when physical combat was inevitable. Nevertheless, this has not yet come to mean that social animals can bluff their way up the ladder. Very few animals are capable of this subtle type of deception, and none could maintain it for a long period under pressure.

The confidence displayed must be real confidence. This means that it must always be affected to some extent by earlier successes and failures, and physical strength will always have played its part at some stage in the youngster's slow accumulation of dominance order morale.

The result is that the larger and stronger animals in each herd or flock will generally rise towards the top of the hierarchy. The physically weaker, smaller animals will usually be forced to accept subordinate positions. A glance at any barnyard community will serve to illustrate this general principle. This is certainly not an absolute rule. One of the most interesting facts to emerge from the scientific observation of free-living hierarchical species is that boss monkeys and wolf pack leaders are not necessarily the largest animals in the group. In the final analysis, the leadership of the group is decided by that mysterious quality which the research worker can only describe as confidence or morale. Nevertheless, the larger contestant's visible advantage must have a considerable effect on his opponent's initial moral whenever a confrontation threatens.

When we turn to the human community, we find a similar connection between social rank and body size in the temporary groups formed by boys. Rank order positions in street-corner gangs are normally decided on the basis of fist-fighting ability, where an individual's body size appears to be of surprisingly little importance. But in more sophisticated groups where physical fighting is taboo, statistical analysis has shown that a boy's social position correlates closely with his size and weight and hence with his *assumed* ability in fighting. Whenever an individual's fighting spirit has not actually been tested, it is evidently judged according to the most likely indicator.

The relationship we might have expected to find between rank and body size applies least of all in the adult human community. We cannot assume that large individuals will automatically occupy important positions in society. Nevertheless, the dominance implication of physical strength has taken its place among the many background assumptions which underlie the logic of man's person-to-person relationships.

The modern adult's recognition of the primitive significance of physical strength, as well as its residual authority to settle minor dominance issues, are both reflected in a number of commonplace figures of speech. If you have the good fortune to have risen high in society and if you make daily decisions with far-reaching effects on other men's lives, then you are not merely rich and influential in the eyes of your subordinates. You are also a *big* man with a *big* name, quite apart from your physical dimensions. The rest remain small fry. They are only little men in the scheme of things. Colloquial expressions of this sort depend for their development on a large number of people who share the feelings and attitudes they reflect. Commercial advertisements rely heavily on this semiconscious connection between social importance and body size, and many examples could be drawn from automobile-marketing, cigarette-selling catch phrases. Body size may bear very little relation to rank in an adult human community, but it certainly qualifies as one element in that mental picture of the confrontation to which we all remain more or less sensitive.

When Hector took his brother Paris aside to point out the Greek heroes on the battlefield below the walls of Troy, he had no difficulty in distinguishing them from the rest of the armoured multitude. Homeric heroes all stood a head taller than ordinary Greek soldiers. A thousand years before Homer's *Iliad* was written down, the Egyptians were already practicing a similar size discrimination in their sacred murals. Pharaohs, gods, and priests are easily recognized. They are painted distinctly larger than soldiers and servants. A similar sensitivity to body height probably underlies the fact that among many primitive peoples it is often considered a gross personal affront, or even an offence against the state, to hold one's head higher than the chief's. (In the popular musical *The King and I*, Hollywood made use of this apparently quaint custom when Anna outrages the king of Siam by holding her head above his.) In some historical cultures, each officer of state was required on ceremonial occasions to hold his head a specified degree below that of his superiors. Today we acknowledge the same principle when we speak of looking up to the men we admire and respect and looking down on the lesser men beneath us.

Many psychologists consider an abnormally small stature to be a serious handicap to the individual's emotional development. The social difficulties which a miniature physique presents to an ambitious man and the unquenchable thirst for enough power to override these difficulties are often blamed for the making of political demagogues and industrial tycoons.

It is generally recognized that physical height commands respect, and most people tacitly acknowledge that if you want respect but do not have height you must somehow compensate for the lack of it. Napoleon Bonaparte, who stood five feet four inches tall, is usually named as the classic example of a person whose life was dedicated to overcompensation. Even if Napoleon was not obsessed by his lack of height, the widespread popularity of this theory suggests a considerable vicarious sensitivity on the part of his audience. Evidence of the continuing importance of body size in our present-day society is the taboo against discussing it in polite conversation. The small man's stature is presumed to be a sore point and we steer carefully around it.

Ideally, we would like to compare these conclusions with scientifically verifiable findings. Unfortunately there has so far been little research in this direction, but the small amount that has been done, however, has produced a number of surprising results. A statistical survey carried out as long ago as 1915 showed that height was related to social success in occupations where we might never have expected it to be. The figures showed that bishops were, on the average, taller than clergymen, and university presidents taller than college presidents. Executives in insurance companies were found to be taller than policyholders, and sales managers taller than salesmen. Other surveys along similar lines have shown that a connection exists between body weight and relative social influence, indicating that, on the average, dominant people tend to be bigger and heavier than their subordinates, even if the matching is not nearly so close as it is among baboons and gorillas. A survey of several thousand American soldiers conducted in 1943 revealed that most of them considered a 'strong physique and good bearing' to be among the twelve most important qualities of leadership in an officer. In his book *The Pyramid Climbers*, Vance Packard reports that the trend in American business is to favour 'towering executives', particularly in sales departments where it is considered essential for a man to be able to assert himself over others in their very first encounter.

Of the handful of studies so far carried out in this field, nine conclude that human leaders tend to be taller than the average, two that they are shorter, and one that the importance of height as a factor in leadership varies according to the type of leadership activity. A cross-section of young male groups studied in America indicated that the difference between the height of leaders and the average height of others in the group was greatest in the case of class presidents and athletic captains and least in magazine representatives.

References to body size in everyday slang and in myths and primitive rituals, as well as the slight advantage that above-average height brings in many informal situations – all these demonstrate man's continuing respect for an age-old element in the dominance contest. The proposition that small, very ambitious men strive excessively for a compensatory degree of power supports rather than detracts from this view. Even when they are high on the ladder, they are still cued unsatisfactorily outside their formal preserve. It is presumably this continual stream of minor pinpricks that keeps them striving for godlike status while others in their position would be happy to rest on their laurels. It has been suggested that a major part of this sensitivity to body size may stem from childhood, when parents, who towered above us, firmly established the association of size and authority in our impressionable young minds. An alternative theory is that physical size does no more than make an individual slightly more conspicuous. Whatever the explanation, the facts show that the primitive criterion of size remains one of the factors on which we base our initial allocations of social priority. When all other factors are approximately equal, the big man is more likely to win respect and allegiance. If the small man dislikes this arrangement, the obligation rests with him to redefine the situation.

Physical Contact and Personal Space

A second factor in this complex of cues that elicit confrontation behaviour in human beings stems from the dominance implication of physical contact. Physical contact remains an obvious element in schoolboy conflicts, where claims of dominance are still expressed by punching and pushing one's classmates. Adult society normally succeeds in channelling this effort into more acceptable forms, but physical contact with a possible competitor continues to function rather like a warning signal. An unexpected shove in the back can still be relied on

to bring up sharply to the alert. Although we know perfectly
well that it could have been an accident, we still feel ourselves
precipitated to the brink of a showdown. The primitive significance of physical contact between competitors is simple : it
would normally have meant that the disagreement between
them had reached battleground intensity. Perhaps we still inherit from the distant past a built-in understanding of this implication. Certainly man remains remarkably sensitive to being
pushed around, and he shares this characteristic with other
hierarchical species.

Monkeys use as many as a dozen distinguishably different
gestures of aggression and self-confidence in the course of their
day-to-day behaviour. The gestures involved in a confrontation
over dominance begin with two animals staring at each other.
At the violent end of the scale, an aggressor will resort to
hitting or biting. Then, as dominance is accepted, the animals
turn to wrestling. As the final gesture in this sequence, the
dominant monkey may put a fatherly hand on the other's back
or shoulder; or he may approach and embrace his subordinate
and perhaps chew on his neck, apparently to reaffirm the
dominance relationship in a relatively settled and amicable
atmosphere.

For the mountain gorilla, dominance interactions most often
occur along narrow jungle trails. Here, the dominant animal
will insist on the right of way. Sometimes a higher-ranking
animal will be seen forcing a subordinate to move from a favoured sitting place. Usually the lower-ranking gorilla will move
away at the mere approach of his dominant colleague, but, if
he does not, he is reprimanded by a light tap with the back of
the hand. Again, the serious threat gestures used by gorillas
begin with a stare and end with physical contact such as biting
or wrestling. In fact, one gorilla may occasionally enforce his
dominance simply by barging into another, compelling the
subordinate animal to stand down.

To judge from the behaviour of a wide variety of animal
species, body contact is charged with the emotional overtones
of a dominance contest in every situation in which a competitive relationship appears possible. Punching and wrestling play
an important part in boyhood contests over rank, and such
formal sports as boxing are merely ritualized versions of this
physical contest. It has been suggested that these approved

forms of competition act as safety valves for our pent-up emotions. As spectator sports, they allow many adults to participate vicariously in the excitement of a violent status contest without causing serious damage to the social fabric. Clearly this sensitivity to the physical contact involved in a confrontation has been retained by adult men even outside the sphere of formal sport. An intentional shove in the chest or tap on the face would be interpreted immediately as an open challenge. Behaviour of this sort is fairly rare, but whenever it does occur it can be relied on to elicit some extraordinary psychological and physiological reactions within a very short space of time. Man remains so sensitive to physical assertions of dominance that society has had to impose restrictions on this class of behaviour, and in many communities the simple forms of assault mentioned above entitle the victim to take legal action against the offender.

The confrontation cue of bodily contact retains its emotional significance even in such supposedly friendly actions as a hearty slap on the back. Although a slap on the back is generally accepted as a friendly gesture, it is essentially an assertive act that implies at least equality, if not dominance. This gesture with its implications of affection, is characteristic of a wide category of behaviour in which one person playfully threatens another whom he knows so well that no real threat could possibly be meant. The pretence is enjoyed for the freedom it gives the participants to toy with normally dangerous actions. Among friends, the slap on the back supposedly signifies an absence of all anxiety, but if the recipient is feeling in any way insecure and touchy, the raw significance of the gesture shows through. Unless he accepts the donor's back-slapping rights, he cannot help feeling a little irritated.

Other examples of physical contact suggesting a dominance difference between modern adults include a fatherly hand placed over the subordinate's shoulder (this gesture is also employed by gorillas and chimpanzees) and manual pressure to the small of the back to reassure the subordinate that he may walk through the door first. If the recipient is not prepared to accept the subordinating implications of these actions, he finds them particularly frustrating. Both of these 'hand on the other monkey' gestures imply a benign seniority against which he has no acceptable way of retaliating. In many instances, they may actually have been made benevolently without any thought to the implied dominance assumptions. To take them at their full value and respond defensively would suggest a petty lack of self-confidence.

Since physical violence is the logical climax of a confrontation sequence, the confrontation cue of bodily contact is particularly forceful. In the comparatively sophisticated context of many primate societies, even the mere threat of unritualized contact with a rank order superior is usually sufficient to cause alarm. Physical nearness suggests bodily contact, and so, whenever a competitive relationship seems possible, the mere proximity of another animal may itself be treated as a warning signal that a confrontation is close at hand. We have seen how a subordinate gorilla will usually move out of the way at the approach of a dominant colleague. Monkeys sometimes use an almost formal technique of repeatedly approaching a subordinate as a means of forcing him to move. In the authoritarian baboon society, a subordinate animal will always move out of the way of a dominant animal as they wander across the countryside. This rule of avoidance provides the field worker with one of his simplest techniques for determining the rank order in a free-ranging troop. He merely has to watch the animals carefully as they move past one another. A reliable hierarchy can then be determined on the basis of who gets out of the way for whom and which animal offers non-verbal apologies when two baboons find themselves too close. This acute sensitivity to the threat contained in physical closeness eventually results in a peace-conserving system of *personal space*.

The importance of physical proximity in a troop of monkeys will be apparent immediately to any zoo visitor. The boss monkey often stands out from the others simply because of the undivided attention he can affort to devote to whatever action he is performing. In a small enclosure, he is often the only monkey who seems to take any interest in the inquisitive apes outside his cage. The reason is simple : all the other monkeys in the cage are thoroughly occupied with watching him and keeping out of his way. When the overlord moves, they all look his way and adjust their own positions accordingly. Under natural conditions, the subordinate troop members have far more room to manoeuvre. This results in a considerable decrease in the general level of anxiety. However, the principle of acknowledging the right of one's superiors to a certain quota of personal space remains intact. It is simply observed in a more relaxed and comfortable atmosphere.

Zoologists use the word *equilibration* to refer to the way that monkeys literally keep their distance from superiors. This term reflects the all-important features of balance and proportion within each social group. To understand the situation in any of the ground-living monkey troops, one has to imagine that each dominant animal has an invisible circle of territory around him which moves like his shadow whenever he moves. A boss monkey's personal space will be larger than any subordinate's. If a subordinate wants to intrude on the territory of any of his superiors, he must humble himself, usually by presenting his posterior, or he risks being menaced. Juveniles quickly learn how much personal space they must allow for each of their superiors in the troop and are careful to respect it. A dominant animal's need for personal space expands when he is irritable and contracts when he feels particularly benign. This results in a situation which, according to Michael Chance, gave primate intelligence an opportunity to prove its worth. To adjust to this day-to-day fluctuation, subordinate troop members must become highly skilled in judging how much privacy any one of their superiors needs at any particular moment and at just what point the bowing and scraping must begin.

A growing body of research now indicates that man is at least as sensitive to personal space as are his animal relatives and that his obedience to the law of equilibration persists despite the crowded conditions of city life. Examination of speeded-up film has enabled investigators to record the effort made by people in crowds to avoid bumping into one another or even brushing up to one another too closely. Every individual remains acutely aware of the presence of anyone else who moves inconsiderately close and who might offer a threat to his otherwise comfortable state of mind. Under the crowded conditions of a city environment, an elaborate system of excuses and understandings has evolved to appease the violent emotions that body contact and unpleasant proximity constantly theaten to arouse.

One theory put forward to explain this unwritten taboo against touching other people suggests that it has a sexual origin – that it has evolved in order to deter each man from touching other men's women. But since men often take greater pains to avoid bumping into men than into women, this interpretation appears inadequate. The male's avoidance of women may be a cultural taboo more or less consciously aimed at maintaining the socially important marriage unit. The considerable effort he makes to avoid other men, as in a baboon troop, appears to be the much simpler result of dominance anxiety.

We have already compared the baboon's posture of submission with the ritualized bow we make before high-ranking people. In all known human cultures, whether past or present, no powerful dignitary such as a king or a high priest can be approached without a suitable show of deference. In some cases, we may only have to bow our heads slightly or take off our hats. In others, we may be expected to fall on our faces once or twice and shuffle the last few paces on our knees. Similar acknowledgments of a superior's awesome presence are expected of us when we enter a holy sanctuary. We are obliged to take off our hats or leave our shoes outside the door. Anyone wishing to approach a god is advised to do so either 'humbly kneeling on your knees' or prostrate on his face. When the low-dominance personality approaches a powerful person, he feels the threat of a confrontation closing in on him. In the primitive, mythopoetic mind, any distinct feeling of this sort is perceived as an independent object. The more strongly it is felt, the more substantial it must be. For this reason, the primitive treats his feeling of anxiety in the presence of an important man as a spiritual extension of the great man's power, a mystical force that the dominant man broadcasts about him wherever he goes.

Despite the clear evidence that passes before our eyes practically every day, it has taken science a surprisingly long time to recognize our intuitive acknowledgment of personal space. In his books *The Silent Language* and *The Hidden Dimension*, as well as in many scientific papers, the American anthropologist Edward Hall waged what was until recently a lonely campaign for the recognition of some of the unknown and non-verbal aspects of human communication. Personal space was one of the elements which first attracted Hall's attention, and he approached Harvard's Dr Roger Brown with the suggestion that every individual in a human society unconsciously keeps himself a set distance away from the person with whom he is speaking. At first Brown scoffed at the idea that the ethological rule of personal space should also apply to man, but in his textbook on social psychology he recounts how Hall proceeded to prove him wrong.

When the question of personal space arose, Brown and Hall were facing one another, seated in chairs, a comfortable distance apart. As the discussion of the merits of Hall's theory continued, with both men apparently absorbed in its consideration, Hall imperceptibly edged his chair towards Brown's. Quite unconsciously, Brown confesses, he moved his chair backwards to compensate for Hall's progressive infringement of his personal space. Brown was still totally unaware of the trick being played on him when Hall stopped the discussion and pointed out that Brown had now moved his chair backward several feet, in accordance with what appeared to be a deep-seated need to maintain a comfortable distance from his colleague. (This anecdote illustrates how frequently it happens that the most ordinary and everyday aspects of our behaviour are the very last to receive scientific attention.)

Hall's work sparked off a series of experiments into this hidden dimension of social behaviour. Subsequent research has shown that people invariably react with alarm or embarrassment when others infringe on the invisible territory of space they like to keep around themselves. The act of thrusting one's face abnormally close to someone else's appears to be a widely recognized way of threatening him. Other studies have shown that extroverts move closer to others than do introverts and that they expect others to approach them more closely. Anxious people judge the distance between themselves and others to be less than it actually is, and their estimates are always smaller than those of their less anxious partners. An unusually clear illustration of man's sensitivity to personal space was seen in the transit stations set up in 1945 for newly released prisoners of war. These men had been living for a long time under severely restricted conditions. When they sat down to a meal in the canteen, some of them went so far as to draw chalk lines on the table to define the elbow room they wanted – one way of coming to terms with their deep-seated spatial requirements.

As social animals, we inherit a number of psychological and physiological needs that require us to interact with other people. At times, however, we want to be alone. Presidents and princes can have privacy whenever they want it simply by ordering their retinues to leave. But most individuals do not have the ability to control the movements of other people in this way. Even asking the last guests at a party to go home can be quite difficult. To some extent, man's hard-pressed need for personal space in a crowded society has been met by the legal institution of private property and the ancient invention of lockable doors; but these devices are often not enough to keep the individual entirely happy. Frequently, they are supplemented by some semi-formal recognition of special privileges and relative priorities. One example of such a semi-formal designation of territory underlies the irritation many housewives feel when other people intrude in their kitchens without showing an appropriate degree of deference. The woman of the house characteristically comes to look on the kitchen as her personal territory. Apart from certain common areas such as the dining and living rooms, houses are usually divided into a number of territorial patches, each with its acknowledged proprietor. These areas can be thought of as institutionalized extensions of personal space. When we wish to enter one of them, we signal recognition of the owner's rights by knocking on the door.

Essentially, knocking simply attracts the occupant's attention. We make our presence known and he is then in a position to invite us in. However, we often knock on the door and walk straight in without even waiting for an answer. This indicates the secondary meaning the practice of knocking has now acquired. An interesting experiment conducted by psychologists at Holland's Groningen University has clearly shown that knocking on a door is widely interpreted as a gesture of deference, approximately equivalent to a monkey's presenting, which appears to have been institutionalized in our Western culture.

Originally the experiment was set up to demonstrate how much information about the rank of two men could be communicated without words. It involved a series of one-minute silent films which always featured the same two actors. In each film, one of the men was shown sitting at a desk in an office, looking through a card index. The film then cut to his colleague coming down the corridor and entering the office. Then the two men could be seen discussing a sheet of paper which the second man had brought with him. In each of ten separate films, the actors were carefully rehearsed on how to play their roles in order to give the impression of a different relationship between them. To make sure that their own personalities would not affect the results, they switched roles in a random fashion. An audience of students, managers, and professional people were then shown all ten films. In each case, they were asked to say which man was superior to the other and how widely their ranks appeared to differ.

The audience response showed a close agreement on the ways in which the behaviour of the actor revealed his relative status. It was clear to the viewers that entering the office without knocking indicated that the caller's status was much higher than that of the man in the office. When the caller knocked but entered without waiting for an answer, the two men were judged to be closer together in rank. The caller who knocked and waited for an answer was considered lower in rank than the man in the office; if he knocked and waited until the answer was repeated more loudly, he was judged to occupy the humblest position of all.

The extent to which the caller infringed on the seated man's territory before the conversation took place was also interpreted as a clue to his relative status. If the caller stopped just inside the door, he was judged to be more subordinate than if he walked halfway towards the desk. If he walked up to the desk, his status was regarded as higher still. If he joined the other man behind the desk, the two men were regarded as approximately equal in rank.

This experiment, quite apart from Hall's work, clearly shows that the infringement of another person's privacy is interpreted as an assertive action. As such, it threatens a confrontation unless it is accompanied by a compensatory show of deference. The explanation for man's sensitivity to personal space appears to be basically the same as that for any other primate community. Close proximity is only one step short of physical contact, which is itself a still more explosive signal in the escalation towards a fight.

Eye Power

In our discussion of physical contact, we noted that monkeys consistently give way to their superiors in the hierarchy. In fact, they may avoid doing this by making one of several sub-ordinating gestures that are considered equivalent to moving. A submissive animal may simply look away from his dominant colleague as a substitute for actually moving away, and so a number of authorities in the field of animal behaviour have listed looking away or avoiding visual contact among the accepted signals of a social animal's submission.

Of course, the eyes play a unique role when two animals confront each other in a contest for social position. The steadiness of the gaze and the fine expressiveness of the facial muscles around the eyes display the determination of each animal's challenge. At the same time, each contestant depends on his eyes to record his opponent's response. If the confidence of either animal should fail him for even a second, his eyes will show it. His opponent, sensitive to the slightest facial or postural changes, is likely to respond immediately with reinforced courage. As messages of this sort fly from eye to eye, the gap in confidence may widen so rapidly that the contest can be decided in a very short time and with no suggestion of bodily contact at all. Consequently, it is not surprising to find that a great many social animals include staring at one another in their repertoire of more effective threatening gestures and that a steady, level gaze is a widely acknowledged characteristic of the dominant primate or wolf pack leader.

There is evidence to show that humans, too, place a dominance value on the uninhibited use of the eyes and that they remain potentially disconcerting objects. Generally speaking, eye contact simply suggests intimacy, but the ever-present possibility of a dominance claim lends the gesture almost unavoidable overtones of assertiveness. Freud has commented on the hypnotist's use of his eyes to paralyse the will of his subject and has compared the power the subject feels flowing from the hypnotist to the power primitive people feel emanating from the eyes of their chiefs and gods. Primitive societies throughout the world have collected their superstitious fears of the threatening gaze and various other types of uncontrollable danger into a single awesome conception – that of an Evil Eye.

A man who feels guilty and fears a challenge is often described as having a shifty look in his eye. This description refers to his evident wish to avoid the implicit challenge involved in eye contact. Correspondingly, a direct gaze is associated with honesty, self-confidence, and self-esteem.

All over the world, young children play the time-honoured game of 'staring each other down'. This game involves gazing fixedly at an opponent, who is staring back, until one or the other gives in by looking away. Children apparently do not need to be taught this game but discover it for themselves. This makes it difficult to avoid the conclusion that they intuitively sense the implication of defeat for the one who is first to look away. The expression 'stare somebody down' is clear evidence of a widespread sensitivity to this aspect of human confrontation behaviour.

The human adult never forgets the dominance implications of looking confidently into other people's eyes. What he may lose, however, is the candid understanding of the situation that he enjoyed as a child. Everybody has experienced the small embarrassment of catching a stranger's eye and feeling obliged to look away. Many people will be familiar with the more considerable embarrassment of catching the same pair of eyes a second or third time. Man still recognizes intuitively that it is the privilege of a superior to look him in the eye. As with his primate relatives, it would often be considered an act of defiance, a challenge, not to look away from a superior's gaze. A complication arises for *Homo sapiens* in the anonymous crowds of metropolitan society. Here he meets so many gazes of every type each day that looking away is simply a rejection of intimacy. In this special context, it no longer necessarily implies submission. However, the busy executive who feels no need to assert his gazing rights in the crowded streets loses this artificial exemption when he arrives at his office, his club, or his home environment.

When we turn our eyes away from someone who has been looking at us, we are effectively declining any challenge they might be making. Nevertheless, we are not necessarily submitting to it. The fully submissive gesture takes the form of the downcast eyes we usually associate with blushing maidens and nineteenth-century servants, cap in hand before their master. A ritualized example of this submissive signal was common in medieval Europe, where monks and nuns were deliberately instructed to walk with their eyes lowered to betoken their meek and lowly hearts. Apart from the deference they owed their aristocratic overlords, the god they served was imagined to be so powerful that no man could look upon his face and live.

Mythological beings in other cultures have had a similar sort of eye power attributed to them. A glance from the Greek Medusa could turn a man to stone. Hamlet's ideal man had 'an eye like Mars to threaten and command'. It would seem that every time we lower our eyes from the gaze of a real or magical superior, we obey an ancient ruling on all hierarchical animals. The relatively lone-living cat may enjoy a psychological nature that allows it to stare back unabashed at an angry king, but few fully hierarchial animals could withstand such a powerful gaze. Correspondingly, the commanding glare of the king, the flashing eyes of the prophet, the crazed look of the maniac – all these descriptions refer to the same phenomenon. Whatever the psychological context may be, they all mean that the individual is displaying the age-old primate confrontation stare to an unusually intense degree.

One of the principal differences between man and his primate relatives is man's ability to communicate in the highly complex medium of language. As a result, the way we use our eyes when we speak to each other has no direct parallel in non-human groups. Recently, British and American psychologists have been examining human eye contact under laboratory conditions with the aid of one-way mirrors, cine-cameras, and stopwatches, and they have noted that when two people talk across a desk they look intermittently into each other's eyes. On the average, each person looks at the other from 30 to 60 per cent of the time and, in particular, each usually looks into the other's face whenever either of them starts or stops speaking. Submission to the other person's point of view is signalled by looking down, and the rejection of something the other has said is shown by looking away. One particularly fruitful test situation was the contrived interviewer–interviewee relationship. When subjects felt confident about what they were saying, they spoke fluently and looked the interviewer in the eye. But when the interviewer was instructed to look directly at his subjects all the time, they looked back at him less often. They tended to avoid eye contact especially when they were asked questions of a personal nature on potentially embarrassing topics. One experiment was set up in such a way that the subjects were tempted to cheat with the answers. Whenever this invitation to cheat was accepted, the subject would normally show the very minimum inclination to look his interrogator straight in the eye.

Both physical closeness and staring seem to be perceived as warning signals in the confrontation sequences of many hierarchical species, and studies conducted on turkeys and fowls in close confinement suggest an intimate connection between the two. Dominant birds enjoy a greater freedom to look about them than do subordinate birds, and the discoverers of this phenomenon have given it the obvious label *eye space*. Not surprisingly, this privilege also varies according to different degrees of crowding. When a number of birds are jostled together in a small cage, they stand up against the sides and turn their heads to face outwards, apparently to avoid the anxiety generated by continual eye contact at close quarters. Several experiments with human subjects show a similar connection between physical proximity and the disinclination to catch other people's eyes. In one experiment, the British psychologist Michael Argyle asked his subjects to approach a series of objects 'as close as it is comfortable to see well', in what he had disguised as an experiment on vision. One of these objects was the experimenter with his eyes closed and another was the experimenter with his eyes open. In both cases, Argyle adopted what he believed to be a neutral-to-pleasant expression, but he found that when he had his eyes open his subjects generally preferred to stand with their faces further away. This finding is supported by graphs which show that when people stand only four feet apart they spend much less time looking at each other's eyes than when they stand ten feet apart. Close physical distance combined with eye contact evidently produces a compound effect – suggesting one possible reason why people crowded together in an elevator take such great pains to avoid each other's glances.

If you have ever been in the position of having to search for a friend in a crowded bar or a large room full of strangers, you will know that it is often easy to miss altogether the person you are looking for and walk right past him. One reason is probably the disquieting effect of so many inquisitive pairs of eyes. One American experiment discovered that subjects giving speeches made about 400 per cent more nervous mistakes when they were in front of an audience than when they stood out of sight and spoke from behind the audience. In another experiment, laboratory subjects admitted they preferred to watch others through a one-way mirror rather than a two-way glass panel because no one would be able to look back at them effectively through the mirror. When we realize that any steady, relaxed, unself-conscious stare automatically suggests self-confidence and possibly an assertion of dominance, it becomes easier to understand how the unapologetic 'threat stare' of a large theatre audience can frighten the uninitiated off the stage. Even veteran actors claim they still feel a thrill of suspense whenever the curtain rises. The steady stare of a television camera, which represents the collective stare of millions of pairs of eyes, can paralyse with fright anyone who has had little experience with it.

Among their other revelations, these studies have shown that men and women obey distinctly different eye-contact patterns. While speaking, women tend to engage in more eye contact than men, particularly if they are speaking to other women. The explanation for this is not immediately obvious, since men are usually found to be more dominant than women by other standards of measurement, and they might therefore be expected to behave more assertively. To explain the anomaly, we must bear in mind that the more dominance-oriented male may be more conscious of the rank order challenge which eye contact often implies. For this reason, he would presumably be more concerned with keeping such contact to a minimum in friendly relationships. In this same experiment, it was found that whenever the interviewer was concealed from his subject, the men talked more than they did when the interviewer was visible, but the women talked less. Women appear to feel uncomfortable when they cannot see the person they are talking to because they rely more on visual reassurance that it is their turn to speak. Men, on the other hand, tend to continue talking until interrupted or until the other man's eyes or body movements signal a request to butt in. In competitive situations, men whom the experimenters describe as 'high in dominative needs' looked into the interviewer's eyes considerably more than those subjects who were 'friendly and co-operative' and 'high in the need for affiliation'. They concluded that this was why women, whom they describe as 'higher in affiliative motivation and lower in dominative', were less prepared than men to look the interviewers in the eye in particularly challenging situations.

Winners and Losers

The ritualized pseudo-fight for social status appears to be one more aspect of dominance behaviour we share with other hierarchically organized social species. Nowadays we seldom resort to a full-blown confrontation display in settling our status differences. Man is usually clever enough to side-step such a showdown long before tempers begin to flare. This often gives the impression that adult humans no longer involve themselves in confrontation behaviour. However, by learning to wriggle out of a confrontation early in its development, we are not necessarily eliminating the pseudo-fight. In most cases, we have simply added more steps to the ritual – not only saving the body from injury but saving face as well.

For the sake of greater social harmony, overt confrontation behaviour, has been classified as bad manners in most modern adult groups. However, this does not prevent healthy young males from feeling a powerful need to prove themselves in challenging status contests. To satisfy this need in a harmless way, different human cultures have devised a great many variations on the pseudo-fight theme which we think of as sports or games of skill. A characteristic of these competitions is that the same fundamental rules of gamesmanship apply as in any other animal's confrontation ritual. Contestants must be closely matched or the encounter lacks sufficient challenge to arouse the physiological fight responses. Competition may become fierce, but the rules of the game must always be obeyed. A pseudo-loser must accept his pseudo-defeat and not resort to unlawful means of reasserting his dominance. Of course, the most obvious parallel between the animal show-fight and the human game is the element of knock-out competition. Whatever the contest, whether we play chess or 'chicken', someone must end up the winner and someone else the loser.

Man's competitive games are several steps removed from the grunting and grimacing of a monkey or ape confrontation.

Nevertheless they test the qualities which would have been of central importance in a physical fight – strength, endurance, accurate aiming, vigorous hitting or kicking, and the ability to remain relaxed and clear-headed under the emotional stress of competition. Moreover, urban pseudo-fighters usually experience a remarkable degree of emotional involvement in their supersophisticated versions of the confrontation ritual. Often they are unable to conceal powerful primitive reactions to winning and losing. Many a toppled tennis star has smashed his racket to the ground and stalked off the court to sulk in the dressing rooms. At one time or another, all of us have felt a sense of elation at winning a closely contested game of chess or billiards. Reactions of elation at winning a ritualized fight and of depression at losing it are characteristic of hierarchically organized animals, and the fact that man also responds in this way is possibly the most important single aspect of human confrontation behaviour.

Whatever the form of the competition – whether the rivalries of the stock market or a contest for political leadership – the emotional consequences of winning and losing remain the same. The winner experiences an immediate rise in ego level, a thrill of elation which he inevitably communicates to others through an increase in assertiveness and self-confidence. The loser is overcome with despondency. His social behaviour becomes more than usually inhibited and he may withdraw altogether from social relationships. Schjelderup-Ebbe observed that a bird which had just won a contest against a rival would display its elation by strutting and parading itself, and a bird which had recently been deposed from its position would become 'depressed in spirit, humble, with drooping wings and head in the dust', even when it had not suffered physical injury. Similar observations have since been made on other hierarchical species, including monkeys and wolves – two animal types which give us the best clues for reconstructing the social designs of our own primate, pack-hunting ancestors.

Since so many rank-contesting species appear to experience elation on winning a status contest and despondency on losing, it seems likely that these emotions have served a common evolutionary purpose. Rearrangements in an accepted rank order are remarkably rare in animal communities; but when they do occur, they threaten the cohesion of the group as a whole and hence the survival chances of all concerned. Accordingly, it must always have been important to ensure that any rearrangements that did occur would be carried out as smoothly as possible. In a recent series of brilliant papers, the British psychiatrist John Scott Price has advanced the theory that the two opposite moods of elation and depression evolved as adaptive mechanisms that helped to stabilize changes in the rank order immediately after they occurred and so minimized further friction. The sense of elation which both men and monkeys appear to feel whenever they rise a step or two on the dominance ladder gives them the extra self-confidence and energy they need to consolidate a new position. The loser in a ritualized fight seldom experiences serious physical injuries. What prevents him from immediately rechallenging his victorious opponent is the sense of depression that comes to dominate his mind. As Price has written:

> It is difficult to think of a behaviour pattern more likely to result in adjustment to a lower level in the hierarchy than the sort of behaviour and symptoms we observe in depressed patients. The ideas of inferiority and unworthiness, the withdrawal, the selective forgetting of memories conducive to self-esteem, the loss of appetite and libido: these might have been designed to prevent an individual from desiring and attempting to regain his former status.

To illustrate the primitive function of this depressive response to losing a ritual contest, Price gives us the much simplified analogy of two brothers, both of whom want to take the same girl out to dinner. Instead of fighting over the girl, our two rivals agree to decide the issue with a game of chess. Both are good chess players, but after a long, drawn-out game the elder brother wins. He promptly goes upstairs to dress for the evening, leaving the defeated younger brother brooding over the chess board. At this stage, the younger brother could change his mind and decide that the game of chess was irrelevant. He could choose to disregard the rules, and while his brother is changing he could steal off and get the girl. But whether or not he supports the rules at an intellectual level, he no longer feels in the mood for such a bold adventure. Defeat has demoralized him:

> He becomes depressed and loses his interest in an evening's entertainment; his libido is reduced and the girl appears less

attractive; his appetite falls off and the idea of a large meal is repugnant; he feels unworthy and assumes that the girl will despise him; in any case he has no energy to go out. He becomes anxious and worries about what his brother will do when he gets back. He loses his self-confidence and does not feel that he can cope with the problems of organizing the evening, dealing with waiters and entertaining the girl.

A short spell of low self-confidence would normally give a deposed champion time to habituate himself to the subordinate behaviour patterns that he is now forced to adopt. In this way, despondency or status-depression might be thought of as nature's way of insuring that social animals will be good losers. Price points out that a permanent state of depression is more common among old people than it is among young adults. This may be because it has always been unlikely that older members of the community would regain their positions in the hierarchy once they had lost them. A mild feeling of depression may serve the evolutionary purpose of retiring older individuals so as to allow younger and more energetic ones to take leadership positions.

In this chapter, we have considered some of the physical characteristics and behaviour patterns which play a part in non-human dominance contests – size, strength, the confidence implicit in various forms of physical contact and in certain special eye-movement patterns. We find that these signals also retain a considerable influence on human behaviour during the anticipation of a rank order conflict. Few people can honestly claim that they feel no sensitivity at all to these typically primate confrontation cues. Man's sensitivity to such primitive signals presumably reflects the biologically inherited blueprint of his dominance-deciding disposition. Moreover, he seems to have inherited the motivation to engage in energetic status-deciding contests. To absorb this pre-allocated energy in a harmless way, man has had to design imaginative imitations of the original pseudo-fighting ritual.

Perhaps the clearest evidence of man's continuing sensitivity to the primeval status contest is his spontaneous emotional reaction to winning and losing. In a previous chapter, we noted that every individual normally experiences only a limited band in the spectrum of dominance feelings experienced throughout the community. At the same time, the stability of the community evidently depends on having each individual's level of dominance feeling match his position in the overall rank order. Elation and depression appear to have evolved as means of facilitating necessary changes in the individual from one ego level to another. Depression would typically mark a period of adjustment to a lower level of dominance feeling. Elation normally marks a period of adjustment to a higher level of dominance feeling. Chronic depression presumably accompanies an individual's failure to develop the personality pattern appropriate to a reduced status in the rank order, while egomania describes someone who experiences a degree of elation far in excess of what his generally accepted achievements merit in the eyes of others.

CHAPTER 4

HOW DOMINANCE IS SIGNALLED

Man usually succeeds in keeping his confrontations well in the background. All adult members of the community have learned how to make the hundreds of small adjustments and allowances that are needed every day to keep their dominance conflicts sufficiently concealed. Most of them strike a reasonably successful balance between occasional spurts of self-assertion and the polite show of deference that is needed for amicable co-operation. A few people throw in the towel too early in almost all their social encounters. They constantly give the impression of being a little too anxious, unnecessarily tense, overly concerned with their side-stepping. At the other end of the scale is the dominant man. Untroubled by the prospect of a confrontation, the high-dominance personality stands out as being a little more self-confident and a little more imperturbable than anyone else.

We pay the dominant members of our society the same polite respect they would receive in any other animal society, and we usually manage to do this long before we get anywhere near a confrontation. We are able to identify high-power personalities by simple and usually unconscious signals, such as the penetrating but unself-conscious gaze we recognize as the mark of complete self-assurance.

Not all the confrontation cues described earlier are equally useful as ways of spotting the high-dominance personality in a modern setting. Size and strength may still retain a set of childhood associations in the mind and thus make it slightly easier for a larger man to behave in a dominant manner in most informal situations. However, they cannot be treated as certain indicators of dominance. We cannot automatically assume that if a man is large and strong he will rank high on the social ladder. On the other hand, the status implications of eye contact and body contact have lost considerably less of their primitive impact. A determined look in the eye or a confident hand placed over the shoulder, contrasted with a furtive glance or a deferential keeping of one's distance, can still give us a good idea of the individual's social rank.

We will consider at this point some of the ways in which modern man signals his rank in day-to-day social life. By now we should not be surprised to find that many of these signals which make rank order claims on his behalf in the boardroom and on the golf course can be traced back to prominent features of the confrontation ritual. We will begin by looking at the characteristic body posture and style of movement which together serve to identify both animal and human overlords.

High-dominance Bearing

Domestic cats provide us with a familiar example of the connection between body posture, style of movement, and social rank. Although they have the reputation of being lone-living animals, cats that live in the overcrowded conditions of human cities create 'establishments' within local areas. The tomcats within each of these communities form a hierarchy on the basis of their fighting ability, and a top cat takes precedence over a subordinate whenever they meet. When several cats are confined together in a small space, the postural cues which signal different degrees of dominance can easily be distinguished. The dominant male is conspicuous for his swaggering and strutting, while the other animals in the group indicate their submissiveness by their deferential posture and humble movements.

Neither strutting nor slinking are permanent aspects of any particular cat's personality. They are ways of signalling relative degrees of dominance or submissiveness. Any cat is capable of slinking whenever it feels timid or submissive, and any cat is theoretically capable of the display which signifies top cat. When a swaggering boss cat is removed from a closely confined group, his subordinates may for a time continue to show deference to his memory; but after a few days, the next most assertive animal takes over. Immediately he begins to strut about and display his dominance in precisely the same way as his predecessor did.

This high-dominance swagger or strut has been discovered in a wide variety of hierarchical species. No special skill is needed to spot the dominant animals in a monkey troop. The high-dominance monkey has a characteristically cocky manner, a constant air of imminent aggression. Examples of a similar postural display in man includes the 'delinquency strut' with which a rebellious adolescent communicates a challenge and the arrogant, rolling walk of a Hollywood gunslinger. Real-life gunslingers can seldom have swaggered to the confrontation with the haughty self-assurance that these films suggest, but the worldwide popularity of the Wild West fantasy indicates that these dramatic status-fighters evoke a powerful response in every human audience. The traditional swagger or *sandunga* of the Spanish bullfighter is clearly a stylized version of the same bearing.

In the last chapter we considered the way in which social animals came to decide their contests for rank on the basis of a confrontation ritual rather than an actual fight, and pointed out that, as a result, displays of confidence and potential fighting ability became more important, while less emphasis came to be placed on the strength and skill that were necessary for success when physical fighting was inevitable. In fact, many social animals have gone a step further in utilizing the advantages of display. No social animal will defer perpetually unless he is kept informed of his proper place. One way animal bosses can keep their subordinates in line is by means of the glares and threatening lunges of the ritual pseudo-fight. The more subtle technique to be discussed in this chapter operates on the principle of continuous advertising. This serves a slightly different social function from the aggressive display exhibited in a pseudo-fight; but the confrontation cues to which the species has already been programmed to react are an obvious source of borrowed material. We can see how a top cat's confrontation swagger becomes a permanent part of his social style when he is forced to be almost permanently on the alert. A more instructive example of this postural display can be found in the jackdaw community.

Jackdaws have two distinctly different ways of threatening each other. In one case, a bird draws himself up to his full height and flattens his feathers against his body. In the second case, he takes up exactly the opposite stance – he crouches low and ruffles his back feathers so that he appears as bulky as possible. The first of these attitudes, which makes the bird appear as tall as possible, is normally reserved for disputes over social rank. It suggests aggression and confidence and seems to have been derived from the intention movements jackdaws make before flying up and onto the backs of their opponents. The second, hunchbacked posture signals determination and defensiveness. This attitude will more often be seen when an individual is defending his nesting site against an enemy. In the course of everyday living, the dominant individuals in any jackdaw flock adopt a slightly upright stance as a permanent postural style. This appears to have been derived from the bird's confrontation display, and the result is that very few subordinate jackdaws ever forget their places in society.

Anyone who has watched two human males confronting each other may have noticed a similar distinction in the human confrontation stance. A man may stand stiffly erect with his chin raised and his head pulled back, looking down his nose slightly. Alternatively, he may lower his head, pull his shoulders forward, and stand his ground. As with jackdaws, the attitude that aims for height is usually interpreted as a claim of dominance. It implies confidence in an easy win and warns the opposing party to stand down. The second attitude, where the man seeks to appear as steady and determined as possible, makes no pretence of easy confidence. In fact, it more or less acknowledges a possible disadvantage and signals the individual's determination to stand firm despite unfavourable odds. Among adults, this thickset and defensive posture is not normally associated with disputes over social status but is usually reserved for matters of life-or-death importance. It is the showier of the two attitudes – standing up straight – which man usually employs during conflicts over social rank. As with so many other social animals, the dominant human male appears to incorporate an element of this confrontation stance into his normal bearing. Rather like the high-ranking jackdaw, the dominant man generally expresses an air of self-confidence and a threat of latent ability in an upright carriage and a head held slightly more erect than his inferior's.

In man, as in other social animals, the dominant swagger functions as a blatant challenge to possible rank order competitors. It is more characteristic of gorgeously dressed clergymen parading down the aisle and wrestlers entering the ring than of the same men in the vestry or the dressing room. An upright bearing signals a high degree of self-confidence but without such clear implications of a threat to anyone nearby who refuses to show deference. This basic posture is an essential part of the aristocratic bearing which has been cultivated by dominant social classes in every known historical context. At no time or place in history have the members of an aristocratic caste slouched about their palaces with sunken chests and heads hung low while their slaves performed the dirty work with shoulders straight and heads thrown back. As with his European and Asian counterparts, the Western Pacific chieftain is expected to stand erect, while commoners who enter his presence are obliged to 'walk small', to stoop or to squat. The connection between what we think of as an aristocratic bearing and a feeling of dominance appears to be so thoroughly built into the human mind that an actor with a menial's part to play has only to think himself into the role for a completely humble stance to follow automatically. Nor could any actor in the role of a mighty warrrior hope to convince his audience if he failed to lift up his head and straighten his shoulders.

The posture of a human male in full dominance display has been institutionalized in the universally accepted military bearing. Army theorists long ago noted the fact that this formalized stance has a valuable feedback effect on the soldier's morale. In the first place, a feeling of self-confidence and pride makes a man straighten up his body. Conversely, it seems that the soldier has only to stand erect in this confidence-signalling way to automatically induce a more confident and assertive state of mind. This close connection between a mood of bravery and its physical expression in an upright bearing has several important implications. For one thing, it indicates how deeply a sensitivity to the threatening postures of a pseudo-fight has been programmed into man and his ancestors. It also suggests that both the man who slouches pessimistically and the man who walks erect and optimistically are using their bodies to consolidate their feelings – the first of depression and the second of elation. Kneeling in prayer, bowing before a superior, standing to attention while the national anthem is played – all these physical gestures probably affect the individual performer at a physiological level and help induce the required emotional attitude.

Konrad Lorenz had pointed out that the experience of military enthusiasm automatically tightens the striated muscles and straightens out the bearing. It pulls the head back into the position that signals high self-esteem and causes the chin to stick out. At the same time, the facial muscles form the hero face we come across so often in the cinema and on propaganda posters. He adds that a chimpanzee in the act of defending his band or family with self-sacrificing courage strikes a very similar pose and that anyone who has seen this display will doubt the unique character of human enthusiasm. The chimp also sticks his chin out and stiffens his body. His hair stands on end. He lifts his elbows and rotates his arms outward. This creates the most bulky and formidable impression possible. A reflection of this primitive stance can still be seen in the threat posture of a street-corner thug.

The low-power personality finds it difficult to imitate the typical high-power stance, feeling himself under constant social pressure and constant risk whenever he tries to. He would find it surprisingly difficult to walk down the street in the upright manner of a well-respected public figure because he is anxiously aware of the challenge this posture implies. He cannot escape the feeling that other people would easily see through him. The low-dominance individual would probably enjoy nothing more than to receive the dominant man's share of deference, and he may even dream that, as a result of some implausible adventure, he will win the necessary degree of respect. Without this, he finds that he cannot maintain the all-day, everyday challenge entailed in standing up straight. As a result, to avoid the discomfort of frequent and painful surrenders, he often adopts a slight stoop of the shoulders as a permanent idiosyncrasy. This serves as a standing apology for any social accidents which might be mistaken for assertions of dominance. Since the confrontation is the focal point of all dominance sensitivity, the high-power individual is likely to draw himself up to his full height when a challenge seems imminent. Under similar stress, the habitual stoop we associate with low self-confidence is likely to become more pronounced and will probably be accompanied by several other distress signals, such as fidgeting, hand-wringing, and compulsive talking.

It may not be true in general that first impressions are most important, but in the case of dominance assessments it appears they are. Research workers who have experimented with rank order formation in non-human social species have often noted that an animal's initial behaviour towards a competitor is likely to determine how he treats this individual in all future encounters. The same rule is at least partly true for man. Along with such factors as looking steadily into the other person's eyes, the posture one man adopts at the moment of meeting another is a major factor in announcing the position he claims and in deciding the position he gets. The widespread recognition of this rule is clearly indicated by the fact that so many parents openly encourage their children to stand up straight, even if they do not do so themselves, because they realize that this will make a good impression in later life.

In fact, there is every reason for the adolescent to stoop in adult company. It is well-recognized primate behaviour for the juveniles in the troop to signal their subordinate rank, their disinclination to challenge, and their readiness to take second place. In comparison to the triumphs of his dream-world, the adolescent has nothing to feel proud of yet. Indeed, his parents' behaviour is often considerably less reasonable than his. On the one hand, they order their son to stand up straight like the dominant man they would like him to be. On the other hand, since they are giving him instructions, they are implicitly demonstrating that he is the very opposite of dominant. No wonder the boy reacts with a scowl when a well-meaning adult pats him on the back, saying, 'Chest out and chin up!'

In spite of the way they may rationalize their own rounded shoulders (assuming they have developed this posture and are consciously aware of it) every parent knows that a straight back indicates the pride and self-confidence he would like his children to have. We would never expect a father to encourage his children to stoop. If we were studying the human species in the same impartial way we study other social animals, we would probably be justified in listing an upright bearing as number one on the list of non-verbal signals by which a dominant individual can be identified. Other signals abound, but in most cases this is the first indication we are likely to receive. Some people characteristically hold themselves erect, while others just as habitually stoop. They are not built this way. They are signalling something. Anyone who carries himself in an upright way, particularly when under stress, is displaying contempt for the risk of a rank order challenge. It can safely be predicted that he is a person of some weight, or at least that he claims some weight, in his social involvements. Other people must treat him with respect or they risk the consequences of an unpleasant confrontation. He is evidently prepared to tread much closer to it than most men.

Relaxed Body Movements

For half a century, Hollywood has depicted every man's hero as the slow-walking, slow-talking cowboy. Today's hero of the James Bond film fantasies never blows his cool but remains impossibly laconic in life-or-death situations. Cowboys of the classic type swagger easily towards each other in the clichéd confrontation of a gunfight outside the saloon while humbler townsmen rush from the dusty field of battle to hide in awe behind the shutters. Whether we are dealing with medieval monarchs or television troubleshooters, the display of social power invariably includes an air of relaxation.

Easy and deliberate movements are essential ingredients in the portrayal of proud and powerful men. They are equally sure signs of dominant animal in other primate groups. In addition to their evident self-confidence, dominant monkeys are easily distinguished from their subordinates by their relaxed behaviour. This contrasts strongly with the fidgety and nervous attitudes that mark the pariahs at the very bottom of the hierarchy, who are constantly looking over their shoulders to see where the next attack is going to come from. If a dominant animal shows any sign of tension, this is a clear indication that he feels under pressure and that his position of authority hangs in the balance.

For nine months of 1962, two British social scientists, Vernon and Frances Reynolds, studied the behaviour of wild chimpanzees in what was then Western Uganda. They and their team of chimp spotters spent up to twelve hours a day in the jungle making notes on the daily life of these mild-mannered forest dwellers. Chimpanzees are known for their unusually egalitarian society. Their version of the primate hierarchy is so relaxed that it is often hard to detect. Nevertheless, the Reynoldses noted that some of the adult males stood out from the rest because of their relaxed and confident bearing and their unhurried gait. They recorded several encounters with 'very relaxed males who seemed to have little or no fear of man and who strode about with great dignity and bearing, even to the extent of walking down the main road through the forest one day to have a good look at us and the camera'. They add, 'This type of behaviour was limited to mature greying adult males, but by no means all grey-backed males behaved in this way.'

This intimate connection between dominance and relaxation has also been observed in a wide variety of other animal species. Carl Murchison, another early experimenter in the pecking order field, was struck by the remarkable differences in behaviour between dominant and subordinate roosters:

The most dominant rooster works smoothly and gently. He seldom shows irritation towards his fellows and does his pecking as if it were play. He may be handled easily by the experimenter and never resists, runs away, or struggles. He will stand quietly wherever he may be placed by the experimenter, and gives one the impression that he is adequate for any rooster situation that may arise. The least dominant rooster seems to be under a strain at all times. He is difficult to handle.... He is never adjusted to any situation and continually fills the experimenter's mind with thoughts of murder.

A great deal of anecdotal evidence could be brought forward to support the view that Murchison's generalization about roosters can be applied equally well to man. Remarking on the monkey overlord's relaxed, leisurely, and deliberate manner, one team of social scientists has suggested that we look for these qualities in our leaders as well. Their conclusion is supported by a lengthy American study on the psychological assessment of men. One of the research methods used in this study discovered a high correlation between slow speaking, if not actually slow thinking, and the likely presence of leadership ability.

Only a limited amount of scientific research has been conducted into this connection between human dominance and uninhibited body movements, but the same general conclusion has always emerged. Following Maslow's work on dominant and non-dominant personality types, a colleague, Philip Eisenberg, conducted several experiments to discover the relationship between the feeling of dominance and expressive movements. The method he used involved more than four hundred men and women who were thoroughly tested and cross-examined by questionnaire and self-rating techniques. The results of these tests were matched and were found to agree very closely. The thirty-three most dominant individuals and the twenty-nine least dominant individuals were then selected for detailed comparisons:

In analysis of the walking, dominant individuals tend to swing their arms feely at their sides, and in general exhibit a free unrestraining movement of the body, which is largely determined by the movement of the hips. In addition, the posture in walking of non-dominant individuals tends to be stiff, stilted, at least when under observation. This may be interpreted as indicating again the general feeling of ease and freedom of the dominant individual and the tenseness of the non-dominant.

The dominant man's relaxed appearance seems to be largely the result of his confidence in facing whatever problems are likely to arise. The nervousness we associate with low dominance presumably comes from the individual's lack of faith in himself. He is always afraid that he will not be able to handle the next crisis to develop. The link between unnecessary body movement and a lack of self-confidence is particularly clear in psychiatric patients who suffer from chronic anxiety. They tend to fidget a great deal and to talk very fast. They speak indistinctly and they often stutter. They usually speak first in any encounter. At the other extreme, manic patients stand erect, speak volubly, and communicate a feeling of relaxed self-assurance.

Our first way of estimating a man's rank in the dominance order is by his posture – how straight does he stand? But this easy indicator suffers from at least one significant drawback. Since the high-dominance stance is open to a certain amount of imitation, it is difficult to distinguish clearly between the well-tried possession of dominance and the hopeful claim. A more reliable indicator is how relaxed and imperturbable a given man appears in challenging social situations.

The Display of Face

Man's use of language is often cited to illustrate the great chasm that separates him from other animal species. In fact, this unique human capacity for speech is itself only a starting point, a basic tool in the service of a much greater body of communicating equipment that often goes unrecognized. Not surprisingly, man's more sophisticated techniques of communication constitute a rich soil in which it has been possible for far more sophisticated dominance signals to develop. We can begin to explore the ways in which this potential has been exploited by considering man's unique capacity to assert himself socially through the display of face.

Accompanied by the music of gongs, drums, and shrieking pipes, the procession passes down through the narrow streets to where the mandarin's boat awaits him at the quayside. The mandarin has been a wise and efficient ruler, less dedicated to self-enrichment than his predecessors. Now that his term of office is coming to a close and the time has come for him to take up a new position in another province of the empire, his grateful subjects have determined to give him a parting gift he will treasure for the rest of his life. The gift is the 'umbrella of the myriad people' – a huge umbrella made of crimson silk which can now be seen flashing in the sun as it is carried high above the sedan chair in which the mandarin sits. The umbrella has been signed by scores of local citizens and bears the simple statement: 'He protected us because he loved us'. Since it represents the spontaneous admiration of the people he has ruled, this great red umbrella means more to the official than the praise of his superiors, more even than the praise of the emperor himself. When he dies it will be preserved by his descendants among the most prized of family heirlooms. For the present, as the procession winds slowly downhill through the city, the usually stern and imperturbable visage of the mandarin glows with benevolence. On all sides the people chant their grief at this loss of so virtuous a leader. Others, admiring the rare splendour of the occasion, whisper: 'What face he has got today.'

The Chinese idea of *face*, while of little value in detailing the dominance behaviour of chimpanzees or baboons, is extremely useful in describing the more subtle dominance interplay of any human community. Chinese society may have progressed further than most in rationalizing the concept, but essentially the same concern for face may be found in every human society throughout the world. The face is the most obvious part of the body to use for symbolizing the dominance value of the intricate personalities we present to one another. We might also speak of a man's bearing when trying to describe the degree of dominance conveyed by his manner, but this would usually be taken as a more superficial description. There is some evidence for believing that the word face originally meant expression; only later did it come to include the permanent physical structure. The fact that the word for face carries the same idiomatic meaning in many different parts of the world certainly indicates how heavily we rely on our facial expression to communicate our rank order feelings. When we use the word to describe this special aspect of inter-personal communication, we might best think of it as referring to a dominance-sensitive mask which the individual holds out in front of himself to inform others of the respect he claims to deserve.

Men who are admired and deferred to and who successfully assume a high degree of dominance may be said to have a lot of face. Men who are given no respect and who claim none for themselves may be said to have little or no face. Since most social groups contain people who would probably like to be credited with more face than they assume, a new field of opportunities for dominance competition opens up. A contestant in the face-to-face encounter may gain face by introducing information into the conversation which raises other people's estimates of his power and sanctity. Conversely, he may lose face by overstepping the rules or by giving away information which reveals that his earlier claims to face were either fraudulent or innocently misleading. A contestant may try to gain face by introducing information that is detrimental to the face put forward by somebody else; in such a case, the gathering becomes a battleground of digs, squelches, and barbed wit. If an attacker completely discredits the face of another, he may be said to have pulled him to pieces or to have shown him up, and the victim can be expected to appear shamefaced. If his downfall came with dramatic suddenness, others may later tell of how his face fell. If a defendant in such a struggle parries an accusation successfully, he may be said to have outfaced his attacker. To be considered socially skilful, to be considered completely equipped and in no need of special consideration, it is essential to be able to save one's face under all circumstances.

Of course, it would be a mistake to think that all the activity in every face-to-face encounter is concerned with winning and losing points. People are generally considerate of one another's personal feelings and take trouble to avoid hurting others. The human brain is so constructed and conditioned as to be extremely sensitive to other people's expressions of embarrassment and discomfort. Because most people feel pity for anyone placed in an embarrassing position, they often use tact to save another person's face. Apart from this altruistic motive, several other considerations must be taken into account. The social group will seldom be a completely random collection of individuals. Often some common characteristic holds them together, and loss of face for one individual may well undermine the claims to rank which he shares with all the others. Two or more persons may be linked by ties of friendship, so that a degree of shared face is involved. Friends may often lean on one another's show of respect to support their own faces, and this again means that a loss of face for one individual threatens a loss of face for his allies.

Even without these special contracts, an irretrievable loss of face for someone who lacks sufficient poise to protect himself may lead to his breaking away from the group in distress. Such a disruption in the ritual order would reflect badly on either the social skill or the magnanimity of all. The need to maintain a harmonious atmosphere, to which all participants must contribute for the sake of orderly, mutually advantageous communication, leaves only a small part of the face-to-face interaction free for competitive displays. All these considerations ensure that face-making and face-saving are carried out in such a way that serious wounds are rarely inflicted and that socially disruptive incidents almost never occur. Victors and vanquished alike are required to manage their victories and defeats in such a way that the ritual order never breaks down.

Sometimes events occur that throw serious doubt on somebody's claim to face. But it does not necessarily follow that a pack of ruthless attackers rushes in to take advantage of the victim's vulnerability. Far more often the result is an embarrassed exchange of explanations or apologies, requests for clarification, and expressions of understanding. The most securely dominant group member is most likely to act to preserve other people's faces: he has least to win and most to lose by collaborating in a breach of the rules. Like the dominant baboon, the dominant man is inclined to protect vulnerable subordinates. Vicious attacks and open mockery are usually confined to groups dominated by irresponsible adolescents and are all but non-existent in adult company. In adult groups, the vulnerable are often far less vulnerable than they feel.

Anyone who hopes to enjoy the high ego level associated with a large amount of face must live up to the high expectations others have of top-ranking individuals, for it is almost impossible for the individual's own evaluation of himself to remain consistently out of alignment with the opinions of others. To maintain that magical aura of authority which the primitive perceives as mana, the dominant man must avoid all types of behaviour which are considered taboo. In this way, the individual's integrated sense of personal pride and honour binds the men with most face to the protection of those with the least. Men who aim high will therefore behave considerately to all who are not fully equipped to defend themselves and will exercise tact towards any man when he is down. Typically, the individual who makes no effort to save his own face would be dismissed as shameless. Those who unfeelingly share in the defacement of others are denounced as heartless. The very fact that heartlessness almost invariably implies shamelessness demonstrates the strength of the obligation that is generally placed on dominant men to save others' faces and preserve the ritual fabric of the gathering.

This is the most sophisticated arena we have yet considered in which social animals may be found fighting their way up the ladder with ritualized thrusts and parries. Although most of the activity in any stable social group will be of a co-operative nature, in all but a few cases there will be some margin – greater or smaller – for face-to-face competition. The fundamental rule is that virtually every social performance we stage involves a wealth of face considerations and therefore implies a certain statement of dominance or subordination. Certain categories of face behaviour are reserved for dominant men and demonstrate their dominance, while others are characteristic of subordinates and serve to signal subordination.

Boasting, or big talk, is the most obvious example of an assertive display of face. In Chapter 3, we pointed out that sophisticated societies have suppressed such forms of dominance displays as slapping people on the back or waving a fist in their faces. In view of this, it is not surprising to find that in many modern contexts verbal boasts are considered bad form. Nevertheless, straightforward bragging has long been accepted practice in many societies throughout the world where dominance displays of every kind are more freely tolerated. The classic example of a society that not only permits boasting but requires it is that of the Kwakiutl Indians, who live on the rich Pacific coast of North America. Dominance competition among the men in Kwakiutl society traditionally takes the form of giving ostentatious gifts and holding extravagant banquets with whose splendour contestants shame their rivals. The following is an example of the boasting song that accompanies such a self-glorifying feast:

> I am the first of the tribes,
> I am the only one of the tribes.
> The chiefs of the tribes are only local chiefs.
> I am the only one among the tribes.
> I search among all the invited chiefs
>   for greatness like mine.
> I cannot find one chief among the guests.
> They never return feasts,
> The orphans, poor people, chiefs of the tribes!
> They disgrace themselves....

Although such egotistical self-applause would be considered distinctly abnormal in modern Western society, it would be wrong to think it completely foreign to our own historical tradition. Ramses II of Egypt stands out from most other Egyptian god-kings for the enormous energy with which he promoted himself throughout the land by means of great stone images of his ideal self. The Assyrian conqueror Esar-Haddon, son of the biblical Sennacherib, applauded himself in these words: 'I am powerful, I am all powerful, I am a hero, I am gigantic, I am colossal, I am honoured, I am magnified, I am without an equal among all kings....'

The absence of all boasting is described as modesty. In its simple form, modesty is a type of face behaviour employed by individuals who desire to be well accepted everywhere. The modest man controls the information he conveys about himself so that others realize he is claiming less face than he might justly take as his due. This is acceptable because it indicates to others that the individual is not entering the lists himself and can therefore be relied on as a fully co-operative ally. On the other hand, when a contestant insists on claiming much less face than he is considered to deserve, others are made to feel uncomfortable. Such false modesty is often used as a way of fishing for compliments. The falsely modest person places his audience under an obligation to give him the face which he has refused to claim for himself. If they were to accept that his acknowledged achievements merited so little respect, they would by implication be acknowledging that their own claims to face were fraudulent.

A certain degree of modesty seems to be a characteristic of modern society and appears to be closely related to the egalitarian ethic of our industrial way of life. The conventional explanation given for modesty is that those who stand out from the common run should not hurt others by emphasizing their dominant status. Boasting is suppressed in the interests of maximum co-operation and group solidarity. But, from the individual's private point of view, the motive for modesty is often much simpler. He fears that he might otherwise be jeered at as a braggart or that he might attract a challenge that would topple him from his perch. Either way, he risks losing more face than he could gain. In fact, much modern modesty is only guardedness and not, as our traditional religion would have it, morality. The differences between Kwakiutl champions and modern American businessmen may be more apparent than real. Many varieties of only thinly disguised bragging are still very much with us.

One of the most remarkable forms of boasting ever to develop within our European cultural tradition was the quiet brag of the Protestants – the very practice, in fact, from which our modern egalitarian modesty derived. For centuries, this institutionalized brand of false modesty flavoured the whole of European society and it left its imprint across the world. Since the Protestant saw his own modesty as a virtue, he could not help but be tempted to pat himself on the back for it. If everybody who restrained himself from boasting took pride in his self-restraint, knew perfectly well that others admired the quality also, and went to great lengths to express this modesty in his dress, the behaviour can hardly be called humility. Similarly, we might argue that much of the apparent modesty of successful men in the modern commercial world is simply careful play. Everyone is expected to see through the mask of modesty to the swaggering Kwakiutl brave underneath. If only they could be certain of their defences, we might still find many modern men who would agree with Ramses II of Egypt and King Esar-Haddon that boasting is only foolish when it cannot be supported by the facts.

It might be argued that the comparatively guarded displays of modern-day ladder climbers cannot be fairly compared to the loud-mouthed bragging of a primitive warrior. Reflecting, as they do, real achievements, they should not be considered boasts. However, this point of view is founded on a misunderstanding of the social function of boasting in a primitive community. An important consideration in the primitive's boastful display is that it must not lay him open to a successful challenge. It is this that makes boasting such an exacting art. The highest honours are separated from utter humiliation by only the thinnest dividing line. Often boasting takes place with the framework of appropriate ceremonies. Typically, the individual recites his claims to glory one by one. At first, each claim receives an affirmative chorus from the audience. But as the claims become progressively bolder, a sceptical note creeps into the chorus of admiration and approval. From this response, the boaster can judge where he must draw the line. Such a ceremony, by laying the attractions of glory out in the open, inevitably inspires ambitious men to greater effort. At the same time, the need to avoid overstepping forces the boaster to make quite sure of the exact size of his achievements. It would be wrong to confuse this licensed display with *empty* boasting. The seemingly immodest arena of the primitive bragging competition is no place for megalomaniac delusions. Apart from its value as a standard format for precise communication, this apparently extravagant claim of face helps ensure that the community will operate in a moral and responsible way. The successful bragger gets his glory, but from then on he is obliged to live up to his boasts and to avoid all forms of behaviour which are below the standard he has claimed for himself.

The Definition of the Situation

The business of gaining face, or at least maintaining an established degree of face, plays a compelling, though undercover,
role in everyday relationships. During the first few moments of
an encounter, each participant must adjust his face to fit in
with the faces initially put forward by everyone else. Every
participant in a social group generally attempts to edit information about himself in such a way that others will credit him
with the highest possible degree of face. This normally leads
very quickly to the establishment of a working agreement,
which we describe by saying 'the ice has been broken', and
which a sociologist would describe by saying that all the
parties had collaborated in establishing a common definition of
the situation. The compromise thus reached may not support
exactly the degree of face which each individual expected or
hoped for. But everyone pays it lip service as a temporary basis
for co-operation.

While the situation is being defined – to use the sociologist's
language – many people experience anxiety, which they reveal
in nervous smiles and awkward silences. This anxiety is characteristic of dependent individuals who feel unsure of the
amount of face they will be given by others. It is also during
this period of mutual evaluation that the dominant man usually makes his claims to face – since it is far easier to secure a
high degree of face at the beginning of a social encounter than
it would be to upgrade oneself afterwards.

The first few words or gestures of the person who initiates an
encounter inevitably imply a number of restrictions over the
activities that follow. He may make sweeping demands for
face; he may indicate that he does not wish to have any say in
determining the way the situation is defined; or he may even
request that the situation be defined as one in which he plays a
subordinate role. In his response to this first package of information, the recipient adds another wave of definition to the
situation. He may reject the first man's implied judgments; he
may passively agree with them; he may accept them with certain amendments. Every subsequent move in the interaction
automatically reinforces and modifies the temporarily agreed
upon background against which every participant is expected
to tailor his face. To the subordinate group member, this pro-

gressive definition of the situation usually seems to take place by itself in a way completely beyond his control. He will almost never try to redefine the situation once it has been clearly settled, and, if he finds himself credited with less face than usual, he will either put up with it or else make some excuse to leave. To the dominant man, the rules that govern the procedure seem extremely accommodating. His words and his attitudes have such an impact on the others that he finds he can usually define the situation almost any way he wants. We might state as a general rule that the dominant man signals his claim to rank by strongly initiating his own choice of definition of the situation. Proficiency in this field is referred to by encyclopedia salesmen as control.

Because we tend to assume that all dominant men are the products of an urgent desire to dominate, we often overlook the fact that many men are gradually pushed up the dominance ladder by a large body of willing subordinates who never feel confident enough to define a social situation with a few positive strokes. Gradually, and often quite unconsciously, the self-assured individual adjusts to the fact that he is regularly cued to declare the tone of a gathering and to define its limits and objectives. Time and again, he finds that until he does so the event never gets started. Accordingly, he learns to take the responsibility for getting the party going, and he grows accustomed to the fact that his remarks will be taken as checks and guidelines to the authorized trend of the conversation. Even though he may feel no personal desire to control other people, he finds himself seduced into assuming a dominant role.

In informal groups, there is usually a wide variety of ways to define the tone of the gathering. Even the most formal situations offer some degree of flexibility. The prevailing definition may be broad enough to permit teasing and poking fun or it may be tight, with everyone expected to treat everybody else's face with a maximum of care and respect. This flexibility works to the dominant man's advantage. Because he is the one who defines the situation, he is able to dictate a tone to the gathering which suits his present mood and permits him to play the part he feels like playing at that moment. The dependent personality feels obliged to fit in and even to change his mood to accommodate the leader.

The dominant man feels under considerably less pressure to

follow an approved script. He feels freer to *ad lib*, to experiment with unfamiliar performances. If his experimentation occasionally results in sudden dead ends, lame denouements, or mild eccentricities, that normally does not matter; he is simply perceived as colourful, picturesque, or informal. The dependent individual is so concerned with security that he finds little opportunity to indulge in such self-exploration. He may feel that he has too little surplus energy to invest in playful self-construction. In a sense, he therefore suffers from a stunting of personality growth. Over the years, the cumulative effect of the dominant man's freedom to explore and experiment is that he not only appears to be colourful and multi-faceted, he actually becomes so. To the extent that his personality is constructed rather than discovered, he develops not only a set of expressive routines but an internal self which complements and corresponds to them.

This freedom for self-expression explains several other reliable high-dominance indicators, such as the ability of the securely dominant man to give face to others, in apparent disregard for his own personal interests. This ability is often interpreted as a mystical quality of selflessness, characteristic of great statesmen, generals, and religious teachers. The man with little self-assurance finds this sort of behaviour impossible. In addition, the dominant man's ability to define the situation in any way he chooses makes it possible for him to express a degree of psychological distance from his colleagues whenever he wishes – for example, when he wants to avoid appearing partial to any of several subordinates. For the dominant man, a social encounter generally involves choosing among several masks, rather than claiming and defending a single, perpetually threatened face.

Subordinate Roles

Although the rules for claiming and maintaining face explain the most subtle self-assertive displays, they have only limited application to an analysis of self-subordinating signals – displays at least as elaborate as those used in the struggle for dominance. To understand the more imaginative of these deferential gestures, however, requires that we first discuss the concept of role.

When we turn to this most sophisticated aspect of human communication, we take a great stride away from the comparatively simple signalling systems used by other animals. Perhaps this is not the giant leap from a mechanical to a spiritual world that men have often imagined it, but it is a very big step. The intricate roles we adopt in our interactions with one another consist of great packages of structured information passed backwards and forwards by every physical means available. Using the word in a simple sense, we could say that other animals also perform such roles as those of mother, pupil, or leader. But when the word is used to describe human inter-action, it usually implies a much larger and more elaborate behaviour pattern. The various roles that an individual learns to play as he grows into a socialized adult constitute major components of his particular personality. It is the role performance for which human language often seems little more than a lifeless tool, and it is the role performance which gives human dominance signalling its unique degree of graciousness.

Initially, the word role seems to have been derived from the roll or scroll used by actors while learning their parts; only recently have the social sciences appropriated the term. There is no hard-and-fast way of precisely defining a role when it is played offstage, but it always involves a more or less standard-ized script with numerous built-in restrictions and obligations. Different social scientists use the word in slightly different ways, but generally speaking a priest or a hostess would be considered a role player, while a cigarette smoker would not. Being a cigarette smoker does not commit a person sufficiently to a standardized set of attitudes and behaviour patterns, while being a priest or a hostess does.

Role playing offers both the individual and the society many advantages that the simpler forms of communication cannot. The elementary dominance signals used by other animals may often be combined with one another to convey a composite message or sentence. When we notice that a dog or a monkey is behaving submissively, we are recognizing several different physical signals that the animal gives off simultaneously in response to a particular emotional condition. By finely grading and combining different elements in such signal clusters, the fully socialized adult monkey can communicate quite subtle shades of meaning. The roles played by human communicators represent a powerful extension of the same principle. After a few decades of practice in the subtle art of role playing, we may need only to observe a small part of another man's total repertoire to construct a rough model of his whole personality and to predict how he will probably react to some hypothetical situation many years in the future. In fact, there is very little of what we think of as another individual's personality that we do not construct out of the roles we have seen him play. We might go as far as to define the word face, as we have been using it in this chapter, as the collective term for all those aspects of an individual's role playing involved in dominance signalling.

The human capacity for role playing has an obvious evolutionary value as a means of co-ordinating individual effort within a community. But why do we, as individuals, continue to confine ourselves within such stereotyped patterns? A social psychologist would probably say that we all feel a need to define our relationships with one another as precisely as we can. We want to know exactly where we stand and what sort of behaviour we can expect from others. Consider how much more difficult it would be to get through the day if we did not perform familiar roles. Complicated social interactions become easy to handle when we have a script to follow. If we had to *ad lib* our way through every dialogue, most social occasions would be quite strained and embarrassing. Perhaps if we were much brainier creatures than we are, we could enjoy establishing entirely new relationships at every encounter. As it is, the carefully worked out roles we play, like the thoroughly practiced faces we present to others, help us to dress up our many social needs in ways we have discovered are fairly sure to lead to satisfying complementary responses.

This explanation for why we act out familiar roles may hardly seem necessary if we think only of the individual involved in assertive displays. But the importance of these fundamental motives becomes clear when we turn our attention from dominant role playing to the roles performed and the faces presented by subordinates. If the prime motive for role playing were to display dominance, we might expect the subordinate personality to do everything possible to avoid presenting himself as a self-effacing stereotype. But, in fact, since he feels comparatively insecure, in no position to experiment or take chances, the subordinate's role playing and face-work are both very closely circumscribed. While the self-confident personality feels free to break new ground, the dependent personality is seldom prepared to leave the safety of his thoroughly rehearsed script. Consequently, he appears to others as a comparatively colourless and unimaginative person. In so far as he seems totally predictable, there is not a great deal to him. This relationship between a severely stereotyped performance and the colourlessness of the performer is particularly evident if we contrast the relaxed and often playful face worn by the dominant man with the self-presentation of a very submissive role player – a flatterer, for example.

When the free-ranging baboon troop settles down and relaxes for its midday siesta, informal grooming-clusters tend to collect around the dominant males. Subordinates are evidently attracted to the dominant individuals and attempt to interact with them to the accompaniment of appeasing displays. The gentle manipulation of a dominant animal's fur evidently puts him in a benign mood and encourages him to tolerate a subordinate's presence. Not surprisingly, this approach is often used by subordinates to curry favour in high places or to work their way closer to a well-protected source of food. Highly ritualized versions of this same courtly performance have been common in human society throughout history. People of power and prestige characteristically have been surrounded by bands of flatterers who depend on this stereotyped self-effacing performance to maintain their positions in the intimate circle. The formal enactment of this traditional role has now fallen out of fashion, but in less formal contexts we still use much the same technique as baboons for keeping in favour with our betters.

Although a modern industrial society has little use for formally appointed flatterers, man's devotion to the part is illustrated by its survival in many primitive societies. Perhaps the most remarkable example of institutionalized flattery in a primitive society can be found in the traditional performance of a Samoan 'talking chief'. Essentially, the job of the talking chief is to mediate between the administrative or sacred chief and his people. Audiences are held in the open with the stone-faced sacred chief on one side and the rest of the population sitting a respectful distance away. Between them is the talking

chief, a combination of master of ceremonies and public relations man. At no time may anyone address the sacred chief
directly. All communication must pass through the talking
chief, whose job it is to boost the sacred chief's prestige by
making continual, exaggerated claims for his wisdom and
power.

Of course, a certain amount of flattery can be mutually expressed without arousing any undue attention. Much of what
we think of as civil behaviour consists of two persons' ritually
ingratiating themselves with one another. We may find it
amusing to watch two adult males who have to walk through a
series of doors together slip into the routine of alternately
offering each other the privilege of going first with a play-
acted, 'After you, Mr Sales Director.' More substantial displays
of mutual flattery are less common, and, except among the
famous, this type of exchange quickly becomes stilted and loses
much of its force. This is due partly to that hangover of humility we inherit from the undercover champions of the industrial
revolution and partly to the credibility gap that begins to
yawn. Flattery must have a fairly solid basis of truth or it risks
being interpreted as sarcasm. Beautiful women may be suscept-
ible to a large show of flattery in the course of a seductive
encounter, since they can easily believe it. But plainer women
will often find that much flattery irritating. Most people feel
proud of at least a few of their personal qualities, and they may
therefore feel they deserve a limited show of appreciation. But
as soon as the safe quota is passed – whenever they feel they
are being given more face than they can justify – they are
likely to accuse the other person of misbehaving. At this point,
the flattered party may protect himself by stopping the interaction and making a joke of it, with a remark like, 'All right
then, how much can I lend you?'

The exact amount of flattery that one man feels he deserves
from another will obviously depend on the dominance relationship between them. Most men would expect to receive
more flattery from an obsequious hanger-on than from a close
colleague and friend. Correspondingly, a string of praises from
someone who is low in our estimation would tend to be valued
less than even a small compliment from someone whose
opinion we prize. This illustrates a very basic rule: dominance
sensitivity is particularly acute between close equals on the

rank order ladder – in man's sophisticated face arena just as much as in the unsubtle world of jackdaws. To the degree that the flatterer's self-effacement reflects a credible estimate of himself, his praises are taken as a matter of course and elicit little emotional response. The emotional reaction triggered by compliments expands rapidly as the rank of the flatterer approaches the rank of the receiver. When an acknowledged superior touches his hat to the eager ladder climber, this is another matter altogether. The smallest gesture of this sort from a man with a lot of face brings with it all that exhilaration and elation which can be expected to accompany a rise in status in any other hierarchical species.

False modesty marks the man who is fishing for compliments. Flattery marks the man who is fishing for favours. False modesty consists of taking an unacceptable degree of face away from oneself. Similarly, flattery consists of giving a more than acceptable degree of face to another, and we find this performance characteristic of the individual who puts a high priority on affiliation at the expense of self-esteem. Because most people are eager to be confirmed in a face that confers more prestige on them than they are accustomed to, flattery can become a powerful tool in the hands of a skilful social strategist. The flattered party feels good as a result of the improved self-image the flatterer has helped him construct. At the same time, he becomes dependent on the flatterer for regular confirmation of this more than ordinary degree of face. As the relationship settles into a well-practiced network of exchanges, the manipulator is able to make increasing demands for time and money or social introductions from the person he is flattering, since the latter now has the problem of maintaining the degree of audience approval to which he has grown accustomed. Most men who climb high on the modern ladder of wealth and titles know how to avoid becoming dependent on flatters and may accept the unwritten contract the flatterer offers to a limited extent. However, the majority of people are wary of any form of ingratiation and are themselves reluctant to flatter anyone who might qualify as a competitor – they equate such behaviour with deference. Instead, they are more inclined to discredit each other's achievements rather spitefully, and they feel tempted to attack whenever they hear a close rival being complimented. An intuitive understanding of the laws of the face arena tells them that compliments have a way of pushing others above themselves and encouraging rivals to step up their claims to face.

Of course, flattery is only one of a wide range of well-recognized subordinate performances. Next door to the flatterer lives the joker. Like the flatterer, the joker's daily round consists very largely of ingratiation. Often the same individual may alternate between the two parts. Since both performances involve a very similar degree of face, it has never been difficult for the jokers to turn to flattery or for flatterers to add a little jesting to their line. There is nevertheless a small difference between the two which usually makes the joker a more desirable type of hanger-on and therefore generally gains for him an extra ounce of face.

A clever joke has a way of dispelling tension and anxiety and brings with it a sense of well-being and brotherly communion. People who laugh together at the same joke feel a sense of belonging to the same group and of sharing a common relationship to the world outside. Shared laughter indicates that everyone is happily agreed on a common definition of the situation. Comedians are probably right in feeling that the amount of laughter their antics trigger is a fairly good index of how well liked they are by their audience. Apparently, it is difficult to find a joke funny if it is told by someone we dislike intensely. If the joke is simply too funny to resist, then the act of laughing at it almost forces us to reconsider our reasons for disliking or distrusting the performer. We are all prone to the infection of a happy laugh and normally feel warmly disposed to those who spark us off. This is the psychological reaction for which public speakers aim when they preface their hard-hitting oratory with an amusing but often barely relevant anecdote. Similarly, telling jokes and making people laugh can be used to win affection in ordinary day-to-day relationships. For many people who employ this friend-winning technique, playing the comic becomes a habitual style. Anyone practiced in the art of winning applause by losing face will usually find a social niche awaiting him.

Occasionally, a skilful and high-ranking role player will use the joker's script in order to save face after a slip, preferring an agile quip to such appeals for mercy as the explanation or the candid apology. But we are concerned here with the individual who builds his whole performance and personality around the joker's role. Like the flatterer, the joker is a fairly stereotyped character in the drama of face-to-face relationships. We might even think of him as playing an archetypal social role – he crops up in almost every possible context. Sociologists conducting an extensive survey of Chicago boys' gangs in the 1920s noted that many of the 1,313 gangs they studied contained a generally recognized funny boy:

> Like the jester of old, the 'funny boy' is tolerated in spite of behaviour which might otherwise be insulting. His irresponsibility is generally excused because of its humorous possibilities. This type of behaviour is sometimes the result of an attempt to compensate for some trait – such as a high-pitched voice – which gives undesirable status in the gang.

The funny boy's part, like the flatterer's, has often taken an institutionalized form. Through the ages, monarchs have found it politically expedient, as well as entertaining, to employ a court buffoon in their banqueting halls. Often the jester was chosen for his unusually childish ways so that his comments could never be taken as a challenge to anyone's face in a serious rank order context. Idiots, like children, are excused as socially naïve. A jester who had any sensitivity for his job provided the court with a welcome distraction whenever the atmosphere between the king and his powerful subjects became strained. The court jester's part has now been replaced by other institutionalized forms of the funny-boy role. First there was the circus clown; then came radio and television comedians whose forte was offering cutting social criticism from behind the jester's mask. At the non-institutionalized level, the court buffoon is still represented by the informal comics and joke tellers who can be found in almost any cocktail party clique. Unlike the person who resorts to self-effacing humour only occasionally, the man who builds his whole personality around this type of face display characteristically develops an amusing range of facial expressions, comical gestures, and ridiculous ways of speaking.

The funny-man role is normally adopted by an individual who has resigned himself to a low-ranking niche. For several reasons, the high-dominance personality is unlikely to indulge in it. As a rule, the dominant individual feels himself under relatively little pressure to restrict his spontaneous responses;

consequently, he is not especially sensitive to that element of humour in many jokes which stems from their tension-releasing qualities. He may make off-the-cuff witty remarks or tell anecdotes he himself has found amusing, but he is unlikely to go to the lengths of learning a list of wholly artificial jokes for subsequent recital simply for the purpose of appearing cute in the eyes of some. To the naïve observer, the funny man may at first appear comparatively high ranking, and the irritation his wife displays as her witty husband takes the stage may seem incomprehensible. The cocktail party joker's technique is often polished, and he seems confident and unself-conscious. At times, he is granted an impressive share of group attention. But this initial appearance of high rank is illusory. When he takes the stage, he does so with the implied preliminary announcement: 'O.K. Look at me everyone. I'm now going to be funny.' He is licensed to assume a high-dominance manner as part of his act. But the joker has openly acknowledged everyone else's right to cheer him or jeer him as they see fit. He has signalled a promise to accept whatever face the audience cares to give him. Those in his audience who might otherwise have taken offence at his assumption of high-dominance behaviour recognize that he offers no serious threat to the faces they present.

The flatterer and the joker are two examples of ways in which a subordinate can arrange the personality he projects to continuously signal his inferior standing in society. Boasting is a straightforward example of the way a dominant individual adapts his social behaviour to convey the very opposite message. Between these extremes, there exists a world of imaginative characters all projecting their own slightly different outlooks on society and all signalling more or less standardized degrees of face. It will be some time before social psychologists can produce even a rough map of the great variety of ways in which skilful role players fulfill the age-old obligation to constantly signal their rank. Nevertheless, there is one other fairly standardized performance which no discussion of human dominance signalling could justifiably omit. This is the face put forward by the arguer. Argument is a role performance comparable to boasting or to flattery, but its usefulness as a dominance signal is more complicated. The complications stem from the fact that a heated argument between two contestants in the face arena is simply a linguistic pseudo-fight. The argument is perhaps the most common way in which an agreed-upon definition of the situation disintegrates, gradually allowing the sophisticated role-playing ritual to collapse back towards a crude physical fight.

A friendly discussion falls under the heading of exploratory talk. The declared aim of a discussion is to exchange information and ideas, and if a disagreement arises the generally accepted purpose is to arrive at a mutually satisfactory conclusion. The anatomy of an argument reveals something quite different. An argument and a discussion may often begin in the same way, but an argument, in this colloquial sense, is a discussion in which the competitive element has been allowed to get out of control. The participants in an informal discussion are physically relaxed. Courteous respect is paid to the opinions of everyone present and to the sensitive faces attached to them. But if one impatient player goes a little too far in his attack on another's face as a means of gaining or saving face for himself, he invites an argument. The invitation is accepted when the victim of such an attack refuses to dodge or simply parry the thrust and instead punches back. In effect, a challenge to step outside the ritual prescriptions for safe competition has been offered and accepted. Once the initial moves have been made, the intensity of the contest nearly always escalates. Anyone so unskilled as to slip into an argument when the definition of the situation is cool is unlikely to be able to stop himself from sliding further once things get heated. As each contestant takes the initiative, he aims to win the audience over to his point of view. If he can do this, he gains face or at least cuts his losses. The audience will have implicitly upheld his claim to authority. The defendant of each attack has the corresponding point of view forced on him. If the audience continues to reject his judgment and hence his right to have the final say, he remains precariously balanced on the fringe of the group, someone who perhaps should not be there at all.

We all know how difficult it is to remain cool-headed when someone challenges our views in an arrogant tone of voice, implying less than the minimum respect we consider due to our face. Accordingly, unless he picks on an exceptionally skilful and self-assured player, the ever-ready arguer usually gets a rise out of the person he challenges. With infallible intuition, both aggressor and victim then slip into the new definition of the situation, in which winning and losing face at the other person's expense are overruling considerations and in which fewer and fewer holds are barred. It soon becomes obvious that the earlier definition of the situation as a co-operative search for a mutually satisfactory answer has now become the thinnest disguise for a dogfight. The opposition becomes wholly enemy, to defeat or to be conquered by. Logic gives way to outright accusations, counteraccusations, and decreasingly subtle verbal assaults. Contestants begin to show clear physiological signs that a dominance contest is in full swing. Characteristically, their faces become flushed or unusually pale and their voices are raised to threat level. The extent of this divergence from the original definition of the situation can be gauged from the reaction of the audience. Spectators interject sharply on half-understood points and may even begin to argue among themselves.

Those individuals who use argument as a regular social device usually will have started out with talents particularly suited to the part, such as a better than average ability to handle logical arrangements of ideas. Certainly they may develop into remarkably skilful arguers over the years, challenging only occasionally and never losing. They tend to become habitual critics who wait on the sidelines until somebody offers such a gaping hole in his defences that the arguer feels he can pounce with inevitable victory. For many of the individuals who adopt this way of dealing with face-to-face interaction, the development has not necessarily taken place consciously. They may not even realize that argumentativeness is perceived by others as an integral part of their personality. Over the years, they have gradually evolved an extensive set of routines, all of which contribute to their argumentative prowess and which gradually take up more and more of the time they spend thinking and feeling about social relationships. Usually they come to reserve their careful attacks for other arguers who rank close to them in the sitting-room pecking order. This bears out the point made earlier that man's sensitivity to confrontation behaviour increases sharply as the rank of the competitor approaches his own. Arguments between certain pairs of individuals may become so predictable that a linguistic tournament of thrusts and parries can be counted on more surely than the weather. Hostesses who are aware of the spontaneous combustibility of such individuals will see that they are always seated far apart at dinner.

How does the dominant individual signal his standing during these guileless verbal brawls in the drawing room? Primarily, he keeps outside the illegitimate fighting – no matter how good he may be at handling logical arrangements of ideas. If he is sufficiently skilful, he may employ some political, slightly self-effacing technique for damping down the fire. But the important point is that he never accepts the new definition of the situation that an argument implies. As in any other competitive game, success in the face arena is achieved by mastering the rules, not breaking them. Generally speaking, the dominant individual is accustomed to expressing himself freely in all but the most formal situations, so he seldom builds up the pressure needed to send him bursting foolishly through the rules. He takes for granted his position of respect in the group and so he sees nothing to gain by winning points in the dominance squabbles going on down below. Like the dominant rooster, he does his pecking as if it were play.

Whenever an informal dominance order establishes itself, we can usually work out the rank of the individuals involved by measuring the length of time they are allowed to talk. As a rule, the most influential person will be allowed the most talking time, although he may not make use of his total allotment. On a busy occasion, those at the bottom of the hierarchy are likely to find that they can scarcely get a word in edgeways. An individual who talks more than others feel he deserves will gradually be ignored. His companions may jolt his face slightly by interrupting him in mid-sentence. If all else fails, he will be excluded from the group in a way that saves him as much face as possible. Most people remain remarkably sensitive to the disapproval of their audience and take great care not to over-shoot their allotted share of the group's attention. Argument can be used as a way of stealing extra time. Like the joker, the skilful arguer may ply his trade simply to gain attention. But this motive is unlikely to apply to the high-power personality. He has all the talking time he wants and he commands all the attention that he wants. The most significant remarks in any discussion are usually addressed to him, and his own contributions always receive more than average consideration. He is flattered most and contradicted least and even his playful

boasting is often accepted at face value. As a standard type of
dominance signal, the face put forward at such great risk by
the arguer therefore differs significantly from those of the
boaster, the flatterer, and the joker. Boasting and flattering may
be taken as straightforward signals – the first of dominance and
the second of submission. Habitual joking usually reflects a
degree of rank order uncertainty. The arguer is clearly anxious
to be credited with more face than he is getting. His behaviour
signals rancorous dissatisfaction.

Dominance and Personality

In the introductory chapter of this book, we stated our intention to explore the extent to which modern man remains a
dominance order animal. In particular, we set out to discover
what degree of influence the primitive rules of the dominance
hierarchy retain in shaping the individual human personality.
We can now begin to give some broad answers to these two
questions.

In Chapter 2, we reviewed man's capacity to submit emotionally to his rank order superiors. We then introduced the
idea first put forward by Freud and later substantiated by Maslow that every individual in a human community experiences
a fairly constant level of dominance feelings somewhere between the two extremes of complete self-assurance and abject,
self-effacing dependence. Along with man's generally acknowledged disposition to climb whatever ladder of social worth is
put before him, these universal human characteristics appear
to be securely lodged in the genetic prescription for our
species.

In Chapter 3, we outlined the part that the man-to-man confrontation plays in modern society and we compared human
confrontation behaviour to its counterparts in other species.
We discovered that man remains emotionally committed to
many fundamental rules of the ritual pseudo-fight that can be
found in any hierarchical venture. We all retain a sensitivity to
such primitive confrontation cues as body size, physical closeness, and staring eyes. As far as man is concerned, these primitive signals may have lost much of their original significance in
the competition for rank, but they continue to affect our
morale in the immediate face-to-face encounter. Finally, we

outlined the theory put forward by John Scott Price that the familiar moods of elation and depression are primitive psychological mechanisms that help the individual adjust his ego level to suit a reshuffle in the hierarchy.

In this chapter, we have examined such simple dominance signals as those contained in body posture or body movements. In this connection, it seems worth noting that a man who holds his back straight and his head up often does so quite unconsciously in response to the high degree of self-confidence he is feeling. This automatic expression of the appropriate signal is characteristic of the instinctive signalling systems on which so many other dominance order creatures depend. The key point is that the signal operates without any need of conscious decisions or futuristic imaginings. The swaggering boss cat or monkey overlord almost certainly has no imaginary picture of what he looks like from the outside. The whole complex of dominance signals he transmits as he strolls among his subordinates is an automatic consequence of the assertive mood he experiences. Worldwide agreement on the dominance significance of various human gestures such as raising the chin or bowing the head argues strongly for the possibility that our sensitivity to these signals is inborn and not merely learned.

When we turn our attention to assertive displays of face and deferential role performances, it becomes more difficult to see how human behaviour could fall within a rigid system of dominance order instincts. These uniquely human forms of dominance signalling stand out from all other types of vertebrate communication for the quantity of imaginative invention they leave to the individual performer. Nevertheless, cross-cultural research suggests that many very basic rules of human role playing and face work are in fact dictated by our genetic design and the physical circumstances of interaction.

No one who takes the trouble to study the Chinese idea of face could fail to be amazed by the precision with which it parallels our own. Chinese role players have precise equivalents for all our expressions regarding the loss of face, gaining face, saving face, and giving face. The Anglo-American may describe a socially insensitive person as 'thick-skinned' to indicate the difficulty of influencing his self-presentation. Similarly, the Chinese will say of a man *'lien-p'i hou!'* – 'The skin on his face is thick!' The Chinese, in fact, divide their idea of face into two broad categories. They may speak of *lien* or *mien*. The first of these might be translated as 'respectability', while the second has the considerably grander meaning of 'honour' or 'fame'. An ordinary shopkeeper who enjoys the respect of his customers has *lien*. To have one's name appear in the Peking *Gazette* and hence have it broadcast throughout China was to possess *mien*. The contemporary Victorian Englishman might have drawn a very similar distinction between the decency of ordinary townsfolk and the special respect due to those whose names were listed in *Who's Who*. The modern American ladder climber confronts the same dilemma as his Chinese counterpart when it comes to deciding how far he should sacrifice *lien* to gain *mien*.

No matter how strange a land we might find ourselves in, we could never confuse the sight of an adult male assertively defining the situation to suit himself with the accommodating performance of an admiring subordinate. The particular cultural tradition into which the individual is born may play a large part in shaping the face he presents and the appropriate self he constructs in his mind. But at the same time, it seems that any particular community's version of the face arena must always be drawn from a genetically restricted range of possibilities.

These faces we fabricate to conceal our weaknesses and to present ourselves in the best possible light to others may at times appear to be the most abstract of constructions. They involve the most self-conscious thoughts and actions, and so they must often seem the least likely parts of human behaviour to be governed by primitive instincts. At the same time, our everyday experience shows that the face an individual wears is intimately bound up with deep-seated dominance-oriented emotions. When we are credited with a little more face than we are accustomed to getting, we spontaneously feel elated. Correspondingly, an individual who finds himself in a situation where he is given less face than he is accustomed to can expect to feel let down or hurt. If this happens frequently, his hurt pride will probably mellow into the long-term despondency colloquially described as 'feeling blue'. In addition, we remain remarkably sensitive to the face expectations and behaviour of our friends and neighbours. An individual who claims more face than he deserves will be denounced by others as 'big-headed', or 'too big for his boots'. Automatically, the 'big head' arouses hostility in his companions. Correspondingly, when we find that a friend is signalling slightly less self-confidence than usual, we automatically warm towards him and lend him moral support. (These simple responses illustrate the way in which society finely adjusts each individual's ego level, and hence his personality, to fit his accepted position in the hierarchy.)

Perhaps the most important clause in this universal role player's rule book is the requirement that all the performances staged by any one individual should convey a consistent and justified degree of face. The more face an individual can justify, the more the definition of consistency expands to accommodate his whims. First, each individual must normally take care that he does not play too varied a repertoire of roles in any one social group. Too little consistency between the fragments of the personality he presents to others will result in confusion and a general suspicion that his performances are insincere. If he does not carry sufficient rank to have these irregularities accepted, he may be asked to 'stop putting on an act and just be yourself' – in other words: 'Present a more consistent face – a face that fits my definition of our relationship.' In addition, he must be consistent from one social group to another. If the individual fails in this respect, he may bump into a man he is accustomed to dealing with in a completely different setting and find that he cannot reconcile this man's expectations with those of his present companions. In such a case, it will soon be rumoured among his close acquaintances that he is two-faced.

The word person is derived from the Latin *persona*, which meant a player's mask or a character in a play. This bit of information serves to remind us of the extent to which we build our personalities out of the performances we stage and the responses we get from our various audiences. We say we are presenting ourselves. In fact, as good a case can be made for the view that we construct ourselves out of those presentations that get the most applause and encouragement from others. In many animal societies, the elementary personalities played out may scarcely develop beyond the point of bare rank order positions. There is some reason to believe that a simple rank order self-estimate also forms the nucleus around which the growing child begins to build his far more elaborate self-image. Certainly man's intellectual capacities make it possible to surround this bare dominance position with the trappings for an extraordinarily subtle drama. Nevertheless, it seems that we are unable to escape from the need to signal our proper rank in almost everything we do. Every role that can be played implies a more or less specific degree of face. It will always be risky to put on a performance that could be successfully challenged. We will almost never be allowed to play roles that carry more face than we are entitled to. Correspondingly, we seldom want to play roles which carry less face than we deserve. As a result, only roles that carry more or less equal degrees of face are likely to become well-practised parts of any single individual's personality. And, of course, whatever sort of self we might have liked to construct, ranking too low in the hierarchy to pull off the performance is the foremost obstacle likely to present itself. Anyone can enjoy day-dreaming about the shining performances he might conceivably stage. But what constitutes a realistic plan of action for the dominant man is merely idle dreaming for the subordinate.

CHAPTER 5

THE HEREDITARY CLASS
RANKING SYSTEM

Until very recently, every large human society of which we have a record has been ruled by aristocrats. These privileged groups of high-dominance people believed themselves ordained to rule. It has always seemed obvious to the aristocratic classes that they were intrinsically superior to the people under their domination, and for the most part their subordinates took this for granted, too. Typically, the nobleman was believed to be a reincarnation of his illustrious ancestors whose successes over the centuries were now proof of his dominant character. Like his father before him, he was born to be master. His subordinates descended from generations of anonymous subordinates. In a society where anyone with no ancestral name automatically deserved no face, they were obviously designed to be servants.

The aristocrat's conviction that he was born a better man than his subordinates was supported by the facts as he saw them. An aristrocrat stood out from his inferiors by his erect bearing, his relaxed movements, his aloofness, his self-confidence, his pride. An aristocrat could never have been mistaken for a peasant. Peasants were humble. They cringed, they shuffled, they averted their eyes from their betters. Every sort of behaviour which seemed to be intrinsically honourable came effortlessly to the aristocrat. He felt a sincere personal revulsion against doing anything small-minded and mean. Peasants appeared to be small-minded by nature, and it could be demonstrated that they were incapable of fully distinguishing what was honourable from what was merely expedient.

Geneticists are still uncertain of the extent to which the many factors contributing to dominance can be inherited. To what extent is the dominant man born that way? But we do know that a lot more went into the making of an aristocrat than the blue blood running in his veins. Different genetic legacies may or may not affect a man's chance of achieving the high dominance attitude of his species; however, he can go a long way towards having this attitude artificially cultivated in him through the sort of training which aristocratic classes have traditionally given their young. To understand how this character-moulding process developed and how it changed the whole design of human society, we have to return to the time when the first primitive forms of aristocracy were beginning to evolve. In particular, we must consider the changes needed to adapt the simple dominance order in a small clan of kinsmen to suit a giant supertribal community.

For the thousands of years that preceded the aristocratic era, man and his ancestors lived in small tribal bands, seldom containing more than fifty to a hundred individuals. No community could grow much larger than this because preagricultural man lived primarily by hunting and by gathering roots and berries. To support the population of even a small modern town on this basis would have required such a huge slice of territory that no centralized community could have developed. Any prosperous band that grew much larger than a hundred members had to subdivide, and its offshoots probably had to dislodge a foreign and weaker tribe for *Lebensraum*.

Modern forms of intersociety competition have become a lot more complicated, with cultures engulfing cultures rather than people displacing people. Nevertheless, for much of human prehistory, selection between communities and selection between cultures evidently took this form of conquest and displacement by small tribal groups. Then about ten thousand years ago, the agricultural and pastoral revolutions ushered in a series of important social changes. The invention of farming and the domestication of various farm animals meant that a relatively small slice of territory could support a fairly large population, and human society began breaking through the simple economic restraints on community size. The ability to produce a regular surplus of food automatically freed some members of the community from the full-time duty of food gathering and enabled them to specialize in warfare, building, pottery, and other crafts. Community size, instead of being a handicap that perpetually threatened starvation, now became a selective advantage in intersociety competition. As a general rule, the larger the community, the better its chance to defend itself and to expand. In the thousands of years that have followed these economic breakthroughs, man has moved his home from tribal villages to mud-brick towns, walled cities and trading centres, and eventually to the seemingly endless carpet of modern suburbia.

For at least ten thousand years, human societies have been subject to a steady selective pressure in favour of larger co-operative units. However, the record of the last few thousand years – which is fairly detailed – indicates that food production and community size could not have been the only factors deciding which community came out on top. Time and again, we find that comparatively small but efficiently organized bands competed successfully against much larger groups whose efforts were poorly co-ordinated. This forces us to modify the simple rule that size meant success. Unless a large social unit was able to function at least as efficiently as its smaller neighbour, its greater size was no advantage. New social designs were needed to enable these swollen communities to operate as efficiently as the old tribal band. To retain the same degree of efficient co-operation in a large society, many modifications had to be made in the simple authority structure that had evolved to suit a small familiar group. New variations had to be invented on the dominance order theme. It was in answer to this need that the hereditary class society and the aristocratic brand of dominance took shape.

The Two-dimensional Dominance Hierarchy

The many advantages of a large population brought with them at least an equal burden of social and economic difficulties. Previously, every individual living in a human or proto-human community had felt a strong sense of attachment to a small band of extremely familiar faces. Much more than in a modern community, the individual's conception of himself and his relationship to the outside world was shaped by the handful of lifelong relationships he established within the intimate group. How was he to feel this clear sense of belonging once he began to mix freely in a community of several hundred thousand strangers? As the human community grew progressively larger, the individual's social environment took on an increasingly anonymous aspect. Accordingly, it became increasingly difficult for him to feel that he had a special part to play as a shareholder in a unique, familylike band.

This need for a new kind of supertribal identity posed a

worrisome problem for the individual group member. But from society's point of view, the anonymous crowd presented a far more serious difficulty. The most important problem facing the community was how to establish and maintain an efficient order of authority within itself now that so much of its population were strangers to one another. As the community gradually multiplied far beyond its original limits, an ever greater proportion of its individual members found it at first difficult and then impossible to arrange themselves in order of rank on the original basis of long personal aquaintance. The most assertive young men would always have been able to single themselves out and establish clear positions. But an increasing majority of the population encountered a ranking problem that the old primate dominance hierarchy was not equipped to handle. If the community failed to solve this problem of efficient control and co-operation, it was likely to end its days as one of those clumsy giants who repeatedly fell prey to smaller but more efficient invaders.

In the most advanced modern industrial societies, this problem of ranking an anonymous community is handled by an extraordinarily complex competitive system which will be described in the following chapter. But for thousands of years prior to this, a solution was provided by the simple method of breaking the overgrown community into a hierarchy of hereditary classes. The enormous expansion of the human community and the development of towns and cities did not eliminate man's commitment to dominance and subordination; instead, it added another dimension. The original ranking principle was simply applied a second time to produce a two-dimensional dominance order. This simultaneously provided a workable solution to the problems of small-group identity on the one hand and administrative organization on the other.

Despite a wide variation in local conditions, all the large communities that have developed during the last five thousand years have responded to the problem of unwieldly numbers by constructing this sort of social layer cake. The large community was divided into subgroups, within each of which the pattern of dominance could be allowed to develop in a comparatively primitive way. At the second level of organization, the subgroups themselves could then be arranged into a hierarchy according to their collective power. This permitted each individual to satisfy his primitive yearning for a clear-cut tribal identity. Admittedly, these tribelike social units could offer only a faint echo of what it must have felt like when the individual's entire world contained no more than a hundred human beings. But even belonging to a servile class was often preferable to belonging nowhere at all. The most important advantage, however, was that the unplaced status-seeker now needed only to find a niche in the structure of his subgroup. Arranging the subgroups into a hierarchy of classes automatically finalized the overall dominance order. Pushed to its extreme capacity, this simple design could now rank millions of individuals along a single imaginary line from a god-king at the top to the lowliest of household slaves or backstreet pariahs at the bottom.

Initially, the division of a large community into a number of subgroups reflected simple lines of association that determined who was most likely to become closely acquainted with whom. Obvious bases for alliance were belonging to the same family, living in the same area, or sharing the same economic interests. Classical Roman society was divided into patricians, knights, plebeians, and slaves. Medieval Europe contained feudal lords, vassals, guild masters, journeymen, and serfs. The hereditary class system the Spaniards encountered in Aztec Mexico contained lords, minor administrators, traders, craftsmen, freemen, and slaves. Like the individual's rank in a simple dominance order, the position of each class in the class hierarchy always depended on similar and fairly obvious sources of political power. The military and religious sectors usually vied for or shared the top position, since these contained a high proportion of the most assertive men of action and the most assertive men of intellect. Trader classes were usually a secondary development, emerging under the shelter of military class protection and tending gradually to usurp power. Whatever the pattern at the top, the people who worked the fields and swept the floors have always ranked near the bottom.

Racial ties, cultural similarities, shared occupational interests – all these provided nuclei around which dominance classes could form. But one of the most important characteristics of this rank order design has been its universal tendency to develop along hereditary lines. Although the current era is one of great social mobility, in the past it was normal for the children of different social classes automatically to develop the dominance feelings and behaviour patterns characteristic of their parents' subgroup. But how could the aristocratic classes reliably produce such a high proportion of heirs with all the evident attributes of high dominance? And how was it possible for the lower classes to produce with equal reliability such a high proportion of offspring who apparently felt, and certainly behaved, like low-dominance personality types?

Without going into the hotly debated question of whether any part of the high-dominance personality can be passed on genetically, we can examine several cultural factors that clearly played a large part in the process of rank by inheritance. Parental care provides the starting point for all of them. The young human being spends nearly two decades of the most impressionable years of his life in a state of psychological and material dependence on his parents, and it is during this dependent period that he uncritically absorbs the greater portion of his social attitudes. (The modern child who boasts to his schoolmate that 'my daddy is stronger than yours' displays an acute intuitive understanding of the way in which human dependents have always borrowed their social rank from the head of the family. He is simply confusing the factors that determine his primitive social status in the child gang with the criteria that determine his father's rank in adult society.) If the child's parent was a dominant person whom he invariably saw in authoritative roles, the youngster would tend to pick up dominant attitudes and mannerisms. If the parent was a low-ranker who was perpetually seen deferring to everyone else, the youngster grew up under an enormous pressure to develop along the same attitudinal lines; instead of being encouraged to develop only those patterns of behaviour that would contribute to a high ego level, he was unremittingly induced to see the world only from a subservient point of view. In all fully developed forms of this two-dimensional hierarchy, the ruling classes explicitly taught their children high-dominance attitudes and manners. Lower class children were trained unwittingly but just as effectively to develop their innate potential for submissive behaviour.

A second important factor contributing to the inheritance of rank stemmed from the fact that the training of a child in dominant attitudes worked its effect at both ends of every competitive encounter. The young aristocrat did not simply admire his father for giving orders in a masterful style. He was encouraged and guided to give orders himself. Every time the child with such backing behaved in a dominant manner, his unsupported playmates were conditioned to regard him as inherently dominant. As the children grew up together, this consistently felt presence of a masterful aura helped to shape the developing pattern of interpersonal feelings and habitual responses they came to establish between themselves.

In addition to growing up in his father's protective shadow, the son of the overlord inherited many physical characteristics and unconsciously picked up many of his father's idiosyncratic mannerisms. Although some of these may have had no intrinsic dominance value, people who had lived under the rule of a single man for half their lives automatically associated his physical appearance and style of behaviour with their mental picture of legitimate authority. Since the training given young noblemen was uniform throughout the aristocratic class, not confined to a single family, the effect of this conditioning was reinforced by the fact that everyone else who mattered was behaving in the same way. At the bottom end of the ladder, the feeling of home-group identification and the practice of intimately shared deference towards an aristocratic class had an exactly complementary effect. Hereditary subordinates were persuaded to develop a uniform acceptance of all aristocrats as self-evidently superior persons.

The modern social scientist sees the hereditary class system as an intricate network of co-operative and exploitative relationships. But to the people who lived in it, it was usually accepted as a divinely or naturally appointed ladder of life. In practice, there was little need for the individual to carry precise subdivisions in mind as long as he was dealing with classes very distant from his own. On the other hand, he was always acutely aware of the smallest distinctions that could be drawn between classes only one or two rungs above or below him on the ladder. It may seem ridiculous to the modern mind that subordinate classes would expend so much effort bickering among themselves instead of joining forces against an exploiting aristocracy. In fact, this perpetual class sensitivity at the close-neighbour level was vitally necessary to the efficient working of the system – as was the absolute acceptance of the authority of the administrating class. Often no perfect dividing line could be drawn between neighbouring classes, but unless frontiers of some sort were maintained in the individual's mind, the whole structure would lose its shape and the machine would run out of order.

Hereditary Class Signals

The research worker can measure a hierarchical animal's social rank by its behaviour in the community – by the way it interacts with its fellow group members. In the preceding chapters, we have explored the extent to which the same elementary rules continue to apply to man. We must now consider the way in which this original pattern was modified by the use that hereditary classes made of artificial aids. For the smooth working of a primitive dominance hierarchy, the high-power individual must constantly exhibit part of his confrontation display so that his inferiors will recognize him and behave in the appropriate manner. For the class system to operate without friction in a large anonymous community, a similar method of signalling was destined to evolve. Human beings have always been as eager as any other hierarchical animal to show off rank. Accordingly, individuals of high social class began to carry with them easily recognized identification marks to give subordinates adequate warning of their position and power. Every status-claiming hereditary class of which we have a record adopted a characteristic range of ornaments and behaviour patterns that excluded lower ranks from its intimate gatherings and contributed to a system of labels for the easy recognition of hereditary overlords.

The same types of signal have occurred time and again with surprising regularity in totally separate cultures. Special sorts of clothing, dialect, commonly used phrases, standard topics of conversation, and automatically implied value judgments – all these have helped to give members of the same class a feeling of subgroup allegiance, while to the outsider they served as the smoke signals of a slightly foreign and hostile tribe. Simple primate signals of dominance and deference continued to play a part in the social life of urban man. They still do. But the system has long been complicated by this second, artificial scale of measurement. When two city strangers sized up each other, they learned to look not only for the signs of primitive dominance but also for any traces of behaviour that indicated the other man's hereditary class. This enabled each of them to estimate in a moment how they should behave towards each other.

One of the easiest and most efficient ways of ensuring the instantaneous recognition of dominance in an animal society is for each animal to maintain a continuous visual display of its status. The monkey overlord signals his claim to authority by swaggering and strutting. In some species, he may also grow a luxurious mane of hair or develop colourful patches of skin on the face or genitals as soon as he has adjusted psychologically to his dominant position. Human societies have also made use of visual display to signal class membership, reserving certain colours of clothing and certain kinds of body ornament for the exclusive use of the dominant class. In fact, every large strati-fied community of which we have a record has used clothing as a class tag – a label each individual wrapped around himself before he left his home in the morning to identify the class to which he belonged. If he wore a higher status label than the one to which he was entitled, he risked being denounced as an imposter, and in some cases he was sentenced to death.

One of the earliest hereditary class societies known devel-oped in the Nile Valley approximately five thousand years ago. Archaeologists point out that in ancient Egypt the nobility must have stood out sharply from their inferiors because of the clothes they wore. All ancient Egyptians dressed lightly be-cause of the hot climate. But the lower classes wore fewer clothes than the upper classes, and their clothes were often quite different in design and may have been made of inferior materials. Those who could claim no rank at all may have spent their days completely naked. During much of the Roman Empire, only the highest public officials were allowed to wear purple, and the patrician dressed quite differently from a member of the lower classes. In medieval France, special materials were reserved for the use of the aristocracy, and no middle class man or woman was allowed to wear precious stones or crowns of gold and silver. In England, as in France, what was the expected attire of the upper classes was for-bidden for the men and women who earned a living in the towns.

While Europe was still passing through what we now call the Dark Ages, an extraordinarily sophisticated version of the hereditary class system was in full bloom in China. Although the distance that separated China from the Near East and India prevented her from borrowing more than the basic elements of their cultural traditions, the signalling system the Chinese developed followed much the same pattern. A man's clothing was as much an indication of his rank as the size and the style of his retinue. The colour and design of the clothes he could wear, the shape of his headgear, and the style of his girdle – all were laid down by imperial decree for each hierarchical grade. Commoners wore black and white, but all men of rank were required to wear clothes that did justice to their station. Officials above the third degree wore purple robes; above the sixth, vermillion; above the seventh, green; above the ninth, turquoise. Only princes of the imperial family could carry parasols of blue green silk.

In the fertile plateaus of Central America, a whole series of colourful hereditary class societies sprang up, flowered, and died, with no interference from the rest of the world. The Aztec civilization of Mexico was still young when Cortez and his Spanish adventurers destroyed it in 1521, and it was still possible for any outstanding warrior to become a nobleman by capturing four prisoners in battle. But already the highest ranking administrative positions were almost invariably filled by the sons of great noblemen, and the whole hereditary class package was clearly on its way. The *maceualtin* (literally, 'the workers') were permitted to wear only white cloaks with no embroidery. Against this plain backdrop, the brilliant decorations worn by their superiors stood out sharply, symbolizing the greater value of the characters within. Only the emperor was permitted to wear a turquoise cloak, which on public occasions was accompanied by a magnificent headdress of green-turquoise quetzal feathers. Throughout the administrative, military, and religious hierarchies below him, every official wore a particular colour and design of clothing and a prescribed range of ornaments according to his rank. To dress above one's proper station was unthinkable to the Aztec. Any man so dishonourable as to do this was ridiculed and in some cases executed.

The fact that the Aztec culture developed in total isolation from the traditions of Europe and Asia is an indication of how easily and widely expressed is the human tendency to display class distinction through colourful clothing. (Even in small, primitive tribes, special ornaments are often reserved for the use of the highest ranking elders. The same principle can be seen in the formation of boys' gangs.) A comparable scale of clothing and ornamentation developed along class lines in the indigenous super-tribal societies of Africa. The feudal society of Japan was elaborately stratified, and the clothes a man could wear were legally determined by his class pedigree, as were the foods he could eat and the design of house he was allowed to live in. The Inca Empire of Peru was divided into four main classes – the nobility, minor administrators, skilled craftsmen, and commoners. The details of every person's life were precisely controlled by law. A man married at the appropriate time, and he could never leave his native community unless ordered to do so by the state. The clothing he wore consisted of a class uniform specially designed and altered when necessary by officials of the central government.

To keep their subgroup signals meaningful and effective, the dominance-claiming classes in any stratified community usually had to go to great lengths to discourage lower class imposters. Herodotus records the passing of restrictive clothing laws in classical Greece. Similar rules were laid down in China and Aztec Mexico. Medieval Europe saw many so-called sumptuary laws passed, ostensibly to stop waste among the lower orders but more probably to check the lower class imitators who kept confusing the established signal system. Despite restrictions of this sort, ambitious members of subordinate classes almost never have been kept under complete control, and the upper classes have usually responded by changing the signal system as fast as was necessary to keep distinctly ahead. This happened in China and Mexico, as well as in the Roman world and medieval Europe.

To the modern mind, this fanatical concern with hierarchical dressing may seem incomprehensible. But to the people who lived under the rule of this ranking system, the reserved styles and materials had an almost religious significance. The emotions they aroused in the subordinate mind were clear and strong, since everyone knew that any breach of the rules would be harshly punished. The religious and philosophic framework of society also supported every detail of the signalling rules. Roman officials, Aztec officials, Chinese officials, medieval European officials – all believed it fitting that the clothes a man wore on the outside should be in harmony with the quality inside. Anything else would clearly result in an unhealthy society where peasants had no respect for the law and junior officials argued with their superiors. The fact that these beliefs seem so exotic to us today indicates how great a psychological adjustment we would have to make to understand what a green robe felt like to the Chinese official who wore it and to the coolie who saw it coming down the street.

In the previous chapter, we touched on some of the ways in which the development of speech provided man with a uniquely fertile medium for transmitting every kind of dominance message. Roughly speaking, there were two ways of harnessing this distinguishing faculty to serve a hereditary class system.

One way consisted of forcing every member of a lower class to begin by acknowledging his inferior quality whenever he spoke to a hereditary superior. By incorporating a declaration of servility into the approved form for addressing an aristocrat, the subordinate classes could be kept constantly reminded of their proper place in the scheme. A well-preserved example of this method can be found today in Japan. Japanese tradition still teaches that people fit in by accepting their proper place – a view that was common in Europe only a few decades ago. Like a number of other Pacific peoples, the Japanese have what sociologists call a *respect language*. Every greeting and every social contact must indicate the kind and degree of social distance between men. Every time a man says 'eat' or 'sit down', he uses a different word depending on whether he is addressing a superior or an inferior. In each case, a different 'you' has to be used. Even the verbs used may have different stems. The present tendency, presumably a reflection of the decay of the old class system, is for these rules to become mere formalities, But clearly this distinction once played an important part in the operation of Japan's extremely rigid hereditary organization.

Nahuatl, the language spoken by the Aztecs, contained special particular and special conjugations for use whenever a display of respect was required. The suffix *-tzin* was added to the names of noble persons. While *tiyola* meant 'you see', *timoyolotia* would be used when the speaker wished to say 'your lordship sees'. While *timomati* meant 'you think', *timomatia* was approximately equivalent to 'you are so kind as to think' or 'you condescend to think'. *Miqui* meant to die. *Miquilia* meant to die in the honourable way that lords die. This principle survives virtually intact in modern Malay. Here, there are ten different ways of saying 'I' and ten different ways of saying 'you', depending on the rank of the speaker relative to the rank of the man he is addressing.

In Europe, the hereditary class distinctions of a few centuries ago have been steadily disintegrating. However, the relic of an old respect language remains. The medieval French peasant addressed his superior in the second person plural, which is still used as a polite form of approach. A similar rule applied throughout the Germanic territories: a superior would normally be addressed in the third person plural. Both of these devices served to indicate that the subordinate would never dream of presuming an intimate relationship. The subordinate called attention to the fact that the man he was addressing belonged to an essentially foreign community. In addition, the actions of a superior would often be referred to in either the passive or the causative voice: 'When is his new house going to be built?' or 'When is he going to have his new house built?' rather than 'When is he going to build his new house?' In modern English, these distinctions are less clearly defined than in any other major language, but two centuries ago they were still very much alive, and hereditary superiors were often addressed respectfully in the third person to emphasize their remoteness. 'As his lordship pleases' was what the overlord expected to hear when he expressed his desires to a subordinate. By incorporating these declarations of rank into the habitual frame of a respect language, each member of the community was continuously reminded of his hereditary position.

A second way of using speech to separate dominance classes was based on the way members of the same subgroup spoke to one another. It is a mistake to think that the distinguishing features of an upper class way of speaking were deliberately invented to keep subordinates down. Only a minute part of the aristocratic language, if any at all, would ever be deliberately designed for this purpose. The development of a characteristic idiom within a tightly knit subgroup was inevitable and largely unconscious. But as soon as this distinction became available for use as a class indicator, the opportunity was. usually grasped. There is little doubt that the ordinary man in classical Rome could not speak the High Latin in which patricians conversed. For several centuries the English upper classes were distinguished from the English lower classes by the fact that they spoke French. Initially, this was a consequence of the Norman invasion but even into the nineteenth century it was still fashionable for upper class Englishmen to sprinkle a few French expressions in their speech, because France was the cultural leader of the day and French the principal literary language of Europe.

George Bernard Shaw made light entertainment of the hierarchical importance of English speaking habits in his evergreen play about the rise of the cockney flower girl Eliza Doolittle. However, he also made the important point that linguistic training and appropriate clothes were not enough on their own to create an aristocrat. Higgins made the mistake of teaching Eliza all the superficial trappings of the aristocracy, the long-distance signals, but none of the carefully learned social skills needed to back up her class face-lift at close quarters. As a result, he created a freak out of the girl, who was then unable to fit in anywhere. Even in the field of speech alone, far more than the accent had to be learned. The wrong choice of words, the wrong subjects for conversation, ignorance of a great many minor taboos – all these were certain to give the game away. Eliza Doolittle was bound to be found out if she only learned a part of the signal system.

Eliza finally got her pronounciation right. What she lacked was real style. Just as certain figures of speech might be taboo in certain class contexts, a whole range of everyday behaviour patterns and emotional attitudes were either required or forbidden. A sophisticated, high class life-style involved so many particles of behaviour that many years of childhood training were needed to imprint each new aristocratic generation. Characteristically, the aristocratic child would spend most of his youth learning how to behave properly. Then, at the appropriate age, he would be formally presented to the adult contingent of his class and henceforth assume full responsibility for his behaviour. A faint echo of this old pseudo-tribal initiation ceremony can be found in the still recognized coming-out season during which debutantes formally enter society. In all the hereditary class societies we know of, the body of everyday social rules that an individual recognized or failed to recognize served to signal his class membership to others. The signalling systems built around clothing and speech were specialized subsections of this more general technique for keeping classes separate from one another, and neither of them were of prime importance in intimate face-to-face relationships.

Regardless of its rank on the ladder of power, every hereditary class developed a characteristic style of social behaviour. But usually it was only the highest ranking classes that found it necessary to take great pains in bringing up their young correctly. The aristocratic class usually worked hard to expand and maintain its power, and it was invariably the most desirable class to belong to. It was always necessary to restrict the movement of hopeful immigrants from the lower classes more fiercely than that of casual emigrés from the upper crust, who wished to drop down to see how the other half lived. Accordingly, the aristocratic class had more use for a complex and hard-to-learn etiquette. In addition, the lowest classes had to absorb all the least ambitious and least capable members of the community who failed to qualify for any respect at all. To accommodate this considerable group of people, lower class behaviour has always necessitated a far less complicated body of rules and formulae. A third factor was that the lower classes were never wealthy enough to let their children waste years on learning a life-style when they could be earning a living. Finally, members of the lower classes were always permitted to fall back on the rules of a more primitive dominance contest whenever difficulties arose. As a last resort, the rule breaker could be hit over the head with a jug, and frequently he was. The aristocratic rule book, on the other hand, had to maintain unbroken order in a whole community of dominant individuals who were never prepared to lose face.

An elaborate code of etiquette has been a universal feature of aristocratic behaviour in all fully developed hereditary class societies. Just as the orderly steps of the minuet made it possible for a ballroom of elegantly dressed people to move in perfect unison with each other, so the complete social rule book imprinted in the aristocrat's mind was really a tremendously intricate formula that enabled a large number of honour-bound and highly assertive personalities to interact harmoniously. The etiquette of an aristocratic class involved much more than the behaviour a modern man calls politeness. It encompassed every permissible form of social encounter and established the limits within which all behaviour had to be restricted so as to avoid any risk of a confrontation. Like a magic spell, the whole rule book had to be followed to the letter or its enchantment would not work. One wrong step would destroy the illusion that everyone was doing exactly what he wanted to do in perfect harmony with everyone else.

For the lower class intruder with an imperfect knowledge of the code, the high life enjoyed by his betters seemed full of hidden snares, raised eyebrows, and embarrassing silences. He was gauche, non-U, ill-bred, uncivil, vulgar. But for anyone practiced in the art of aristocratic intercourse, social life was a highly ritualized dance where the steps were all known and action followed action with complete predictability. A lifetime of practice allowed the well-bred person to go through all the actions with the detachment of a sleepwalker. In fact, this extreme degree of emotional imperturbabilty was often explicitly required. As long as eveyone kept to the rules and kept his temper, nothing could go wrong. This fact contributed to the atmosphere of perfect ease and self-confidence. At the same time, each player had the assurance that every gesture he made in conformity with the rule book charged him for that moment with sacred authority. It was a display of rank as surely as is the upright swagger of a monkey overlord, and since it was backed by the rule book, it was as unchallengeable as the aristocracy whose banner it upheld. In passing the wine from right to left around the table, the English aristocrat was performing a gesture that he knew would be recognized as a sign of dominance by everyone present. He felt himself involved in a collective display of mastery. The legitimacy of this claim was self-evident. One had only to compare the quality of the guests present with the quality of the servants and to consider the recorded glory of the former's ancestors.

It is the universality of the institutionalized aristocratic life-style that most interests the sociologist. For this reason, the presence of a similar code of behaviour in the youthful Aztec Empire is particularly important to us. When the Spaniards first broke through into this world at the beginning of Europe's sixteenth century, Mexico was the only nation on earth that provided compulsory state education for every child – in a population of more than a million and irrespective of social rank. But already a wide gap had developed between the type of education given to commoners and the education given to the children of the ruling class. The aristocrat's school, the *calmecac*, trained young men for the highest offices of the state and imprinted a body of ruling class values and manners that seems to have differed significantly from what was taught in the common schools.

By far the most important Aztec sport was a strenous and semi-religious ball game that only members of the ruling class were allowed to play. The shared sense of gamesmanship which this encouraged made a powerful subgroup cement. Exclusively aristocratic sports also developed in many other parts of the world. In thirteenth-century Europe, the tournament was a serious form of military training; subsequently, it evolved into a decorative and distinctly aristocratic pastime. Renaissance educators specifically distinguished between noble and ignoble sports. John Locke later advocated fencing and riding because they were 'looked upon as so necessary parts of breeding that it would be thought a great omission to neglect'. The parallel with Aztec life exists even today – a wide range of sports from polo to soccer remain all but legally exclusive to particular social classes.

'Speak in French when you can't think of the English for a thing – turn out your toes as you walk – and remember who you are!' the Red Queen instructs Alice in a satirical echo of the upper class Victorian mother. The present Duke of Windsor recalls how his father Edward VII would frequently instruct him: 'You must remember who you are!' The young Aztec aristocrat's paternal lectures began in much the same way: 'Never forget that you descend from noble forefathers. Never forget that you do not descend from gardeners or wood-cutters. What are you going to be? Would you like to be a trader, walking with a stick in your hand and a load on your back?' The Aztec rulers admired military manners and achievements, praising firmness and self-discipline. The aristocratic ideal was a man who could master himself and who displayed no emotions in public except when and as prescribed by the ritual. He was required to remain reserved and imperturbable at all times: 'One must speak calmly, not too fast, nor heatedly, nor loud.... If you hear and see something, particularly something wrong, pretend not to have done so and be quiet.... Do not be too curious in your clothes, nor freakish ... on the other hand do not wear poor, torn garments.' Like his European counterpart, the young Aztec aristocrat was directed to 'walk quietly, neither too fast nor too slow ... do not walk with your head down or leaning on one side ... or else it will be said that you are an undisciplined fool.... Do not eat too quickly or in a careless manner; do not take great mouthfuls.... Do not use all your fingers when you eat.... If you drink water do not make a noise.'

Synthetic Social Power

The hereditary class system had a spectacular effect on human society. Time after time this ornate structure has held picturesque swarms of people in co-operative order for several centuries without bursting. However, even at its most inventive, it could never do more than produce synthetic dominance. It would be a mistake to think it substituted a radically new design for social co-operation. It brought into existence the aristocrat, the vassal, the peasant, the slave. But if we want to understand how social life looked from these new points of view, we have to remember that, while the hereditary class system changed the face of human society, it left intact most of the invisible circuitry that lay behind. Beneath an ornamental exterior, the fundamentals of man's ancestral dominance order remained unchanged.

At first sight, the new signals of artificial rank that aristocratic classes used to set themselves apart might have appeared to be thoroughly original – cultural inventions that had nothing to do with the biology of dominance. But the motives for inventing them cannot be explained without reference to dominance. Their primary function remained the job of separating superiors from inferiors. A close examination reveals that even in their apparently novel details they often depended on the imitation and exaggeration of primitive dominance messages. The aristocrat was not only taught to speak with an upper class accent, he was also instructed to speak clearly, distinctly, and with the full-toned voice that required comfortably relaxed throat muscles. A confident and erect bearing, relaxed movements, an outward expression of imperturbability – these were universally recognized as essential attributes of any member of a dominant social class. Since these are also the outward signs of dominance in a primitive community, it is not difficult to see how the development and elaboration of high class signals occurred. The ruling class may have been founded originally by a consortium of high-power military leaders. Thereafter, subsequent generations would gradually institutionalize and sanctify all those aspects of the dominant manner which could be described and imitated. These would come to be recognized as signs of good breeding and would then be methodically handed down to each new generation in a socio-religious educational package. The extent to which these new class signals incorporated the old dominance order principles emphasizes the fact that the class system was not an alternative to the old primate dominance order but an elaborate expansion of it. Moreover, the precision with which these signals of high class quality mimicked the outward signs of primitive dominance indicates how thoroughly man's respect for these primitive signs must be programmed into the individual, partly genetically and partly by the universal circumstances of childhood.

The most obvious illustration of this process of imitation is found in the way man adapted his clothes. In view of the enormous variety of ways in which clothing and ornaments could have been used to signal differences in rank, it is remarkable how often the artificial devices developed by the class system made use of primitive dominance laws. As a rule, the male's choice of dress has tended to incorporate those features that emphasize primitive dominance characteristics. It is generally accepted that tallness commands respect, and in fact a great many tricks of the clothing trade throughout the world have been concerned with making ordinary-sized men seem tall. Time after time high-heeled shoes found their way into the masculine fashions of dominant classes. Tall headdresses and ornamental plumes have been used to signal artificial rank in virtually every large society. Familiar examples to the European are the nineteenth-century gentleman's top hat and the headgear of senior officials in both the Roman Christian and

Greek-Christian priesthoods.

The same principle of exaggerating the physical characteristics that suggest dominance can be seen in the wearing of epaulettes and padded shoulders to give the impression of awesome musculature. Another example is the stiffly starched collar, a device that has been used in several other cultural traditions apart from our own. The high, stiff collar gave its wearer an air of authority – mainly by forcing him to hold his head up in a way that signals self-confidence.

Another technique frequently used to help man remember the rank order in the hereditary class structure was the association of the appropriate attitudes of dominance and subordination with the formal terms of a respect language. But if we examine any informal dominance order, we find that all individuals normally speak in a different way and use different words depending on whether they are speaking to inferiors or superiors. If you happen to be a middle-ranker in a boys' gang and you consistently speak to your captain in the same way that you speak to the gang's lowest ranking hanger-on, you will soon be pushed into line by force or else bullied out of the bottom end of the structure. The formal terms of a respect language simply institutionalized a very elementary principle.

The aristocrat's indoctrinated life-style gives us a more subtle illustration of the way the artificial class signals mimicked old dominance order values. We have already noted that aristocratic etiquette involved more than just a list of rules. It included the values, attitudes, and co-operative policies that lay behind the rules, and it involved an uncritical, almost religious respect for whatever was prescribed. All the dos and don'ts of a particular upper class life-style were wrapped into a single bundle and the whole was invested with a generous measure of superstitious awe. Here again we find that primitive biological factors helped to mould every intricate detail.

The English public school system could not in all fairness be considered perfectly representative of the methods used by aristocratic classes to indoctrinate their young, since this style of education only reached its full development in the nineteenth century, when the hereditary class system was already well on its way out. By this time, the public school's main function was to convert the sons of a rising mercantile class into instant noblemen who could then be sent abroad as imperial administrators and soldiers. Nevertheless, the English public school leaves us the best-preserved example of how an essentially aristocratic outlook on life was artificially instilled into generations of young empire builders. It still gives us the most detailed recipe available for the manufacture of synthetic dominance. Every child who attended one of these efficient training centres came out six years later imprinted with the aristocratic etiquette – not only the written and unwritten rules of conduct but also the attitudes and values that converted these rules into a consistent high-dominance life-style.

The method used by the British public school to mass-produce aristocratic administrators followed the psychological principle that tightly cohesive groups all but prohibit delinquent behaviour. Characteristically, the whole school would be divided into several carefully matched houses. House spirit was recognized as the barometer of subgroup loyalty and was methodically encouraged by competitions in which prizes and honours were awarded to outstanding individuals for bringing glory to the house. Through techniques of this kind, the pupil was trained to feel that he shared in a closely knit pseudo-tribe's exclusive understanding and evaluation of the outside world.

The pressures the public school brought to bear on each raw individual it processed have been compared to the psychological techniques employed in subliminal advertising. They operated beneath the level of conscious recognition, subtly moulding the pupil's most personal attitudes and aspirations. He might have fiercely resisted learning the Latin and Greek he thought he was there to study. But, more importantly, he did absorb the underlying ethic that governed his day-to-day social relationships. The desire to fit in with the other boys and the traditions they supported led each new pupil to accept the unwritten rules with blind faith. In most cases, these rules were never justified or explained. They were treated as self-evident moral values, and the principal punishment for breaking them was shame. The dominant man supposedly obeys the rules because he values them personally – not because he is afraid of breaking them and being punished. The appeal to good form communicated the desired outlook to the pupil not by threats but by the implied challenge to emulate an ideal type.

One of the expressed intentions of public school education was to instill in the boys what one sociologist describes as 'a mysterious aura of differentness which distinguishes certain leaders and makes them respected for what they are rather than for what they do.' It would be difficult to point a finger more explicitly at the high-dominance attitude without stripping it of its magic cloak. The sons of bourgeois parents could not have been expected to learn this 'mystical glamour and lordly attitude' from their humble shopkeeper fathers. Under this sophisticated administrator training scheme, however, the sons of bourgeoisie and aristocracy alike learned the same rules of etiquette and the same framework of personal values. The middle class boy strove to be accepted. The aristocrat strove to keep ahead. Every individual the public school processed was familiarized with the type of artificial authority he might one day be expected to handle, along with the aristocratic obligations that went with it. To cultivate a dominant state of mind in the senior boys, they were given a degree of real authority over their juniors and the most promising of the senior pupils were appointed prefects, who were allowed to cane their fags and other juniors without permission from a housemaster. The purpose of this was to train the young empire builder in voluntary obedience to a code of behaviour which would restrain him in later life from doing anything that was not worthy of a man of honour. As an artificial aide to winning the magical aura so necessary in a leader, the prefect was given more comfortable and exclusive quarters along with his artificial rank. This measured application of material distance helped him to simulate and cultivate the psychological distance needed to command the respect of his one-time equals.

Along with these deeply rooted high-dominance attitudes, the public school boy was taught all the elementary behaviour patterns needed to command attention. The most obvious of these was the habit of standing up straight. The aristocratic bearing was taught through the medium of a cadet corps. Here a young student could be told to keep his shoulders back and to hold his chin up without humiliating him. Outside the cadet corps, deportment might never be mentioned so explicitly. [To state the reason for it would in many cases have been self-defeating.] Instead, the senior boys were exhorted to set an example – to carry themselves in a way that showed they were worthy of their rank.

A similar training in the most basic elements of the dominance system lay behind the generally hierarchical atmosphere that coloured every aspect of adolescent life in one of these aristocratic institutions. Firstly, this familiarized the boy with the way in which completely dominant and completely subordinate patterns of behaviour interrelated. Secondly, it stimulated him to make an intense effort for prestige in the precisely defined channels put before him. Every boy in the school was clearly ranked, according to his year, and according to his academic and sporting achievements. This rank decided which peg he could hang his mortarboard on, where he could sit for his meals, where he stood in the morning procession to community prayer, and whether or not he was allowed to wear a coloured pullover or carry a furled umbrella. Sir Winston Churchill, a famous product of the public school system, gives us some idea of how awe-inspiring these schoolboy honours were to the young pupils who had not yet won any. Soon after entering Harrow, and before he had learned to recognize his superiors by sight, young Churchill made a dreadful mistake:

The school possessed the biggest swimming bath I had ever seen.... Naturally it was a good joke to come up behind some naked friend or even enemy, and push him in. I made quite a habit of this with boys of my own size or less. One day when I had been no more than a month in the school I saw a boy standing in a meditative posture wrapped in a towel on the very brink. He was no bigger than I was, so I thought him fair game. Coming stealthily behind, I pushed him in, holding on to his towel out of humanity so that it should not get wet. I was startled to see a furious face emerge from the foam, and a being evidently of enormous strength making its way by fierce strokes to the shore. I fled, but in vain. Swift as the wind my pursuer overtook me, seized me in a ferocious grip, and hurled me into the deepest part of the pool. I soon scrambled out on the other side, and found myself surrounded by an agitated crowd of younger boys. 'You're in for it,' they said. 'Do you know what you have done? It's Amery: he's in the sixth form. He's Head of his House; he is champion at Gym; he has got his football colours.' They continued to recount his many titles to fame and reverence, and to dilate upon the awful retribution that would fall upon me. I was convulsed not only with terror, but with the guilt of sacrilege. How could I tell his rank when he was in a bath-towel and so small? I determined to apologise immediately. I approached the potentate in lively trepidation. 'I am very sorry, I mistook you for a Fourth Form boy. You are so small,' I said. He did not seem at all placated by this; so I added a most brilliant recovery. 'My father, who is a great man, is also small.' At this he laughed, and after some general remarks about my 'cheek' and how I had better be careful in future, signified that the incident was closed.

Whatever else the English public school might have lacked, it did prove successful in supplying an administrative elite to govern the world's largest empire. The prefect in the above anecdote, Leopold Amery, later became a cabinet colleague of Churchill's. In this tale from their school days towards the close of the nineteenth century, both Churchill's and Amery's behaviour illustrate the point behind the public school's appeal to good form. The dominant man's behaviour must be governed by his own imagined ego rather than by pressures and threats from outside. The dominant man takes his authority for granted. He does not normally need to enforce it with aggressive displays and if he does engage in such displays it indicates that he is feeling insecure. This was why the senior boys were given a guaranteed degree of artificial power – to let them feel that they did not need continually to prove themselves. They were encouraged to develop a confident rather than an aspiring social manner, and Amery's treatment of the young Churchill shows how successfully the system worked.

The English public school may not have been perfectly representative of aristocratic educational institutions. Nevertheless, the aristocratic manner was inculcated in much the same way throughout history wherever a hereditary class system developed. Since the ingredients of leadership magic and the logic of face work are basically the same for all people in all cultures, it is not surprising to find that the techniques employed in the English public school bore many similarities to the educational programmes developed for the Aztec nobility and the children of Chinese mandarins. The education of a young Roman patrician also followed the same lines. In all these cases, the attitudes considered acceptable in a nobleman were inculcated through a code of etiquette and appeals to honour and good form. While subordinate tribes and social classes might speak a variety of dialects and even different languages, the administrative elite learned a single aristocratic dialect, cultivated a uniform aristocratic life-style, and absorbed the same high-dominance pattern of social attitudes and values.

Overlord and Underling

Time and time again throughout human history, the hereditary class system developed afresh out of a comparatively simple tribal background. A number of factors contributed to its development in any community that grew rich enough and large enough. Man apparently inherits a pressing disposition to feel himself a bonded member of some intimate tribelike social unit. Simple arithmetic set a limit to the number of fellow group members with whom he could ever become closely acquainted, and a variety of practical considerations such as family ties or shared economic interests decided the lines along which community subdivisions were destined to occur. Inevitably, these separate classes acquired different forms and degrees of power, and a number of factors then pressed for their perpetuation and increasingly clear separation. Although any given community that achieved the economic licence to develop along these lines could have refrained from doing so, its competitive neighbours would have overwhelmed it as soon as they developed a design that handled a larger population more efficiently. In other words, it seems that the eventual success of the hereditary class system was guaranteed by the impartial rules of intercommunity selection. Small communities that managed without it have been swallowed repeatedly by large communities that used it well. As a general rule, any effort to get rid of the hereditary principle altogether either resulted in the collapse of the civilization in question or simply altered the criteria on which the hereditary aristocracy claimed power.

In the next chapter, we will examine the intricate ranking technique that is now taking the place of the hereditary class system and consider the ways in which dominance and subordination are distributed in a modern industrial society. However, it will be a long time before the social scientist and the social engineer can eradicate the deep impression the old hereditary class system has left behind. To understand the extent to which this social design has moulded the human personality, we must recognize how wide the difference was in dominance order moral between the overlord and the underling. The institutionalized difference in ego level between noble and serf was the essence of a social system that ruled the world from the first city-state to the steam engine.

In the primitive tribal context, the adult dominance order developed very gradually out of intimate face-to-face relationships, and therefore each individual's position on the ladder of influence closely matched his level of dominance feelings. Outstanding warriors were proud and imperturbable, while their less successful kinsmen looked up to them for support and guidance. Even in slightly larger agricultural communities in which rank was to some extent inherited, the dominance relationships between neighbours must still have developed gradually in an intimate context, thus permitting each individual's degree of dominance feeling to match his dominance status. As the community expanded and anonymous relationships began to play a significant part in the individual's daily life, dominance itself became depersonalized. The subtle and unspoken relationship between kinsmen who had known each other since childhood was gradually replaced by a formal hierarchy in which the appropriate dominance feelings were attached to each rank order position. In most of the contemporary primitive societies that have not developed along hereditary class lines, no individual will admit to being intrinsically inferior to another. Observation may show a fairly clear ladder of authority and priority, but the myth of equal value and delegated leadership is all but universal. Presumably the same would have been true of our ancestors. This emphasizes the extent to which the hereditary class system depended on consistently inducing an appropriate ego level throughout each distinct class in a giant community.

Most historical instances of a clearly defined hereditary class society conform to what is called a *conquest state*. Characteristically, the aristocratic class is descended from a conquering tribe, and the servile class contains the descendants of the conquered people who accepted serfdom rather than annihilation. Really pronounced distinctions between the upper and the lower classes have probably never evolved in any other way. In such a case, the establishment of class divisions will usually have been a brutal, bloody affair, and it is not at all difficult to account for the extreme difference in initial ego level between the conquerors and the conquered. There then remains only the question of how these extreme distinctions in dominance feeling were maintained through so many subsequent generations of peaceful co-existence. In Chapter 2, we noted how two to three years of conditioning were sufficient to wipe out all traces of defiance in Gestapo concentration camp victims and to induce not merely a willingness but even an eagerness to accept the overlordship of their guards. The living conditions of servile classes kept under aristocratic domination were probably less severe than those in such camps, but they certainly can be viewed in a similar light.

In trying to imagine the everyday reality of life in a hereditary class society, it is important to keep in mind that nobody could remove himself from it psychologically with the intellectual detachment possible today. Anyone who had the misfortune to be born a serf could not even imagine what life looked like to the aristocrat. The aristocrat was equally unable to understand the peasant's view of the world; his ability to view the social order through servile eyes was irreversibly blocked during childhood. The aristocrat and his hereditary subordinate might sleep less than half a dozen yards away from each other nearly every night of their lives. Nevertheless, they were strangers to one another to an extent which very few modern men and women have ever experienced or imagined.

We tend to forget that the ideological beliefs of the period and the way in which the everyday world was interpreted always supported the aristocrat's obvious and apparently natural superiority. On rare occasions, a peasant might rebel and defy the system by throwing an arrogant young prince off his horse or by raping his lordship's daughter. But then the nights that followed would be filled with anxious dreams full of irresistible risk-takings and terrible punishments. Nor would these dreams be interpreted in a modern scientific way. They were not electrochemical patterns in the circuitry adjusting to the day's excitement; they were vivid warnings from above. Everyone was wholly involved in the system. Everyone believed in it and could imagine no other system. Everyone was psychologically chained to his hereditary situation and accepted without question the network of morals and magical taboos that the system threw around him. Members of the very lowest classes might make no attempt at all to compete for prestige. The middle-ranker might devote his life to winning prestige in his own social bracket and might work his fingers to the bone, without ever thinking of fixing his sights on a share in the ruling coalition. As late as the nineteeth century in England, the commoner who made good considered it the crowning achievement of his life to receive a minor aristocratic title from his hereditary overlord. Even the arrogant bandit chiefs who for thousands of years rebelled against aristocratic authority would never have contested the magic legitimacy of the hereditary principle. More often, they would find some way to believe that they were really the ill-used bastards of a noble line. For thousands of years, the hero of the folktale has had to be either an acknowledged aristocrat or one whose noble birth is discovered at the end of his adventures. In this way, his excellence was legitimized and brought into line with reality.

We have seen how this typical response to life in an outsized community took shape along closely parallel lines in Europe, Central and South America, China, and Japan. However, the classic example can be found in the caste system of India. Here a regional variety of what seems to be the standard pattern reached the full flower of its development during the first five centuries of the Christian era. Nowhere can we find a more exact distinction between the way of life enjoyed by a hereditary overlord and the existence suffered by his various subordinates.

Traditionally, the Indian community was sliced up into a great number of precisely labelled hereditary categories which were grouped into several main castes. The *Brahmans* constituted a powerful priesthood, while the *Ksatrivas* were warrior nobles. The *Vaisyas* were merchants, craftsmen, and peasants. The *Sudras* were servants, occupying a very similar position to that of household slaves. In India, the priestly class had successfully appropriated the prime authority once held by the military aristocracy, as is evident from the fact that the military class was generally accepted as caste two. On a day-to-day level, however, these heirs of former warrior-conquerors still enjoyed the most luxurious lives. In contrast, their servants were allowed to eat only the remnants from the master's table. They had to wear his cast-off clothing and they were allowed to use only discarded utensils. Finally, the very bottom category of human life consisted of *pariahs* or *outcastes*. For a modern man to appreciate the outcaste's view of the social order and at the same time comprehend the serenity of a god-like Brahman or the outlook of a mighty noble calls for a feat of emotional gymnastics.

As his label indicates, the outcaste had no formally acknowledged rank at all, and he existed by doing all those jobs which would have polluted the soul of a man of caste. The outcaste might be a hunter, a fisherman, a butcher, a sweeper, or a gravedigger – all these livelihoods normally constituted dirty work in this priest-controlled society. With a motley assortment of others like himself, the outcaste lived in a separate village or in a special location on the fringes of the town. He spoke a degenerate dialect. He was believed to dress in clothes stripped from corpses, and he was allowed to eat only out of cracked bowls and dishes. He was permitted to use only iron for ornaments and jewellery. A Brahman who killed an outcaste incurred precisely the same penalty as that for killing a dog.

The essence of the outcaste's incomparably low rank and self-esteem was understood mythopoetically and seemed so vile that it was certain to be dangerously contagious. In time, therefore, the outcastes came to be referred to as 'untouchables', and of course it was the untouchable's responsibility to keep out of touch. It would be a mistake to think that high-ranking men in classical India were peculiarly insensitive to the untouchables' sad position. Pity came spontaneously. But this pity was an unenjoyable emotion. Insofar as it could be treated as an external object, it was located in the untouchable who elicited it. So the untouchable was often blamed even for the pity he aroused. An untouchable who defiled a man of caste by tarnishing the breeze that blew towards him or by allowing his shadow to touch his superior risked being beaten unconscious as a punishment for his slothfulness. If a man of high caste so much as looked at an outcaste accidentally, he was bound to perform a ritual purification. To protect his soul from infection, he had to turn away immediately, to bathe his eyes in perfumed water, and to abstain from eating and drinking for the rest of the day. Whenever the outcaste left his compound, he took a pair of wooden clappers with him to warn people of his approach – so that they could shout at him to keep away before he came into sight.

Under these circumstances, it must have been a rare untouchable who ever forgot his proper place in society, especially since the ideological religious beliefs of the era provided the social design with moral support. The classical Brahman religion had for centuries taught that the individual soul was immortal and was reborn into a succession of prisonlike mortal bodies. A good deed reduced the number of wretched rebirths ahead, while a bad deed increased the total. Buddhism had introduced the idea that a man who led a well-disciplined and virtuous life would be born higher up the caste ladder in his next life. Those who led bad lives by defying the legal and religious regulations pertaining to their caste would be reborn lower in the hierarchy. Any soul that successfully endured a whole series of pious existences eventually escaped out of the top of the system into the eternal, egoless bliss, Nirvana. Since the Brahman belonged to the highest caste, he was believed to be only one step from this heavenly breakthrough. He had a purer soul than others. He had been born a Brahman because he had a clean record of virtue and honour in past lives. Accordingly, he could no longer be sentenced to death or any kind of torture or corporal punishment. A member of the servile caste had no hope of improving his situation during this life. He had obviously been born with a heavy load of evil deeds to his debit. The best policy for him was to be a very attentive and loyal servant so that next time he might be born as something better. The worst record of all was obviously held by the outcaste. There was a strong possibility that the outcaste did not even have a fully human soul. If he now defiled a man of caste by carelessly drawing attention to himself, his semi-human spirit ran the risk of being reborn next time in an animal.

This ideological supporting structure played a large part in equipping each individual with the attitudes and outlook appropriate to the social position he inherited. It served as a body of semi-rational ideas in the background that gave the underling some sort of answer to his daily complaints. It helped everybody to adjust psychologically to the facts of the social situation. Within a few centuries, an equally ingenious justification of the class system would be taking shape in medieval Europe :

Servitude is ordained by God, either because of the sins of those who become serfs, or as a trial, in order that those who are thus humbled may be made better. For servitude is of great help to religion in protecting humility, the guardian of all virtues; and it would seem to be pride for anyone to wish to change that condition which has been given him for good reason by the divine ordinance.

If we step back again into the framework of the European caste system, we may be able to gain an additional understanding of the wide gap in ego level that separated the noble from the serf by considering the full implications of the aristocratic custom of duelling. Because the European aristocracy was fundamentally a military caste, armed combat was a traditional method of settling rank order rivalries. In the early sixteenth century, however, the man-to-man duel of honour became increasingly fashionable and soon was established as virtually the only arena for settling rank order disputes between men of noble birth. In the nineteen years between 1589 and 1608, eight thousand aristocrats were killed in duels in France alone. This gives us some idea of how fiercely these men defended the honour which justified their pride. Since the great majority of such 'affairs of honour' were not fatal, these figures do not give a true reflection of the number of duels actually fought in France at that time.

Perhaps the most remarkable feature of these duels is the triviality of the pretexts on which they were frequently fought. As often as not, the duel was a deliberately engineered opportunity for the display of character and was entered into almost playfully by young aristocrats eager to validate their claims to face. Consider the self-evaluation of young Francis de Montmorency, comte de Bouteville, who was in the habit of approaching any nobleman of whose courage he had heard, saying: 'I understand, Sir, that you are a brave man; I should like to allow you to prove it – what are your weapons?' Eventually, Louis XIII had de Montmorency executed. When the bishop advised him at the block, 'My son, you must no longer dwell on worldly things. Are you still thinking of life?' the condemned man replied, 'I am thinking only of my moustachios – the very finest in France.' De Montmorency may have been exceptional, but Lord Herbert, English ambassador to the court of Louis XIII, remarked in his autobiography that there was scarcely a gentleman in Paris at that time who had not killed his man in a duel.

In the ideology of the European caste system, only members of the ruling elite were considered worthy of the degree of face which necessitated such a costly ritual as the duel to defend it. The individual who either proposed or accepted the challenge to a duel was not properly supposed to be doing so on his own behalf. He was considered to be defending the honour of his ancestral name and in fact, of course, he was unwittingly supporting the underlying hereditary ethic. All authority in this society was vested in the ancestral name, the lineage. To be born the temporary custodian of one of these illustrious names, and therefore duty-bound to defend its prestige in courtly rivalries, was considered to be the only valid justification for fighting a duel. In whose name did the servant dare to challenge? To be nameless was to be faceless as well. The serf was not entitled to feel proud; he had no honour to defend.

Many people living in the advanced industrial societies of today believe that they understand what a hereditary class system feels like. Many believe they are still living in one and feel morally indignant because they suffered the disadvantages of a lower class childhood. But if the old class system were really alive today, there would be no moral grounds for complaining. The fact that hereditary inequality is now recognized as unfair is proof of the demise of the hereditary system. Ralph Linton, in *The Study of Man*, makes the point that the lower caste Hindu would normally never covet the rank and prestige of his superiors. If he ever envied them their luxuries, it would be in much the same way that he might envy the lot of some other animal species. Modern man remains sensitive to the comparatively faint traces of class distinction which still linger on in a new cultural pattern, but what the real system once felt like is now all but impossible for us to imagine. Hollywood has done its best to reproduce the sensation but has usually failed. A thirteenth-century peasant, viewing a contemporary movie set in the medieval era, would see only a large number of middle class townies, good at enacting the drama of middle class town life, but quite incapable of pretending to be lords or peasants. The aristocrat took his position of authority completely for granted. The social design and its supporting moral structure encouraged him to exercise the high-dominance potential of his species to its limits. Like a dominant baboon, the hereditary overlord was accustomed to spending his time enjoying an extreme form of what a number of modern writers would call positive thinking. The serf was a subordinate for new reasons, but his servility depended on the fullest exploitation of his old primate capacity for subordinate feelings and behaviour patterns. The imagination and initiative the serf might otherwise have enjoyed was strangled by an extraordinary concern for caution and civil self-restraint.

We now look back on the hereditary class system through a fine historical strainer. We try to understand and to imagine the feeling of life in a caste society from a totally opposite ideological standpoint. Often our present educational system selects for our information not the most characteristic aspects of the era but an unrepresentative structure of remarks made by the most precocious of observers and facts which only proved significant in retrospect. If in fact we could travel back in time to a thriving hereditary class society, we would find ourselves immersed in what would seem to our modern eyes a strange and often tragic world of childlike supersubordinates at one extreme and unbelievably self-confident and capricious nobles at the other, with a greater or lesser class of Janus-like middlemen sandwiched in between. One thing that would certainly strike the modern observer would be the almost magical way in which these unfamiliar personality patterns complemented one another to produce a politically stable community. But perhaps the most astonishing feature would be the precision with which every individual's ego level matched his heavenly ordained rank. If for one reason or another sufficient members of a subordinate class rejected the status quo, the magic spell would break. Once a serious ideological rupture had occurred, a political revolution was fairly sure to follow. However, these revolutions from below have not been frequent. Far more often, a hereditary elite has collapsed only in the sense that a foreign aristocracy has conquered and replaced it. When we consider the dictatorial control the hereditary class system had to maintain over the personalities of the millions of people it frequently contained, it has proved overall a disturbingly successful social design. As long as dominance feeling and dominance status remained in harmony, the caste society flourished. As long as each individual's ego level could be made to match his hereditary rung on the ladder, no one was able to visualize any alternative social environment.

CHAPTER 6

THE INDUSTRIAL
RANKING SYSTEM

The fall of the hereditary ranking system has toppled the aristocrat, the overlord who never needed to earn his rank but was carefully trained from birth to display all the behaviour patterns and attitudes of mind which constitute high dominance. A whole category of human societies has slipped below the horizon. Only a dying afterglow remains of what was once a brilliant world of kings and princes, mandarins, shahs, and maharajahs – a world of thrones, sceptres, jewelled robes, and parrot-feather headdresses. But as this old world disappears, new potentates are arising to satisfy man's passion for power on the one hand and his need for charismatic leadership on the other. These are the presidents, millionaires, managing directors – the stars and superstars of the modern industrial dominance order.

Perched high at the top of a multi-layered business hierarchy, the tycoon celebrates his latest business triumph with champagne and cigars when he already has more money than he can spend. Hard-working subordinates develop ulcers in the anxious struggle for a degree of wealth and importance they will never achieve. Millions of people strain their budgets and torture their nerves in an attempt to give the impression that they are more successful than they really are. They talk about success. They envy it. They read success stories; in the movies they follow the careers of men and women who climbed to fame and fortune. All these people are competitors in a new ranking system – the most sophisticated method man has yet devised to create an order of influence and control in a large anonymous community.

To understand how the dominant man achieves his success within this modern industrial dominance order, we must first consider more carefully the way in which his primitive counterpart would normally win his rank in a small tribal band. We must take two steps backward, beyond the hereditary class system to a social design based on the oldest of all dominance order principles: the principle that every individual must earn his own position on the ladder.

Primitive Human Ranking Systems

In a vertebrate society, the dominance order is normally established through physical fights or pseudo-fights between individual animals until a generally acknowledged ladder of proven superiority has been created. The primitive human community is often small enough to permit the use of the same technique, and normally the dominance order among contemporaries in a closely knit band is established while its members are growing up together. But primitive man is an extraordinarily imaginative and inventive vertebrate, and, just as many other social species have eliminated injurious status fighting and have replaced it with some ritualized contest, primitive human societies have developed an amazing variety of methods for setting up an efficient order of rank while at the same time minimizing damage to the community's strength and co-operative spirit.

The Eskimos of northern Greenland provide us with an example of a crude human ranking system in operation. Eskimo bands in this particular infertile region seldom contain more than a hundred members and therefore provide a living example of a small primitive human society. Young Eskimo males score status points primarily on the basis of their hunting skill. In addition, they may win bonus prestige in an all-male competition which centres around the practice of wife stealing. Eskimo husbands are famous for their hospitable custom of lending their wives to their guests for the night. A pretty wife is a status symbol, and to make a gift of one's wife is to make a magnanimous display of property. When an Eskimo wife is stolen, the prestige flows in the opposite direction. Even though the thief probably has a sexual interest in the woman, this interest is only an incidental part of the contest. What is more important is that the wife stealer gains points, while the insulted husband slips down a rung on the ladder unless and until he avenges the insult.

The higher a man's prestige in the eyes of his competitors, the greater the honour of successfully stealing his wife and the more watchful he must be. Wife stealing is such a brazen challenge in Eskimo eyes, that the injured party is honour-bound to confront the thief if he is not to suffer an enormous loss of face. Since serious injuries would represent an expensive loss to the community, Eskimo society has evolved several relatively harmless competitions in which assertive males can settle their differences. At an appointed time, the two contestants will meet to decide the issue with a wrestling match or a battle of song. The spectacle of an Eskimo song battle would probably seem as bizarre to the modern industrialist as a game of golf would seem to an Eskimo. The two contestants confront one another before an informal audience and then take turns hurling abuse at each other in songs they have specially composed for the occasion. The competitor who receives the most applause is declared the victor. This settles the question of honour, while the impassioned mutual abuse works off the aggressive emotions aroused by the process of challenge and counter-challenge.

Throughout history, the socially approved forms of dominance competition have generally developed along lines that do a minimum of damage to the co-operative effort. Any society that squandered its manpower on unrestricted dominance fighting would not be able to compete with its rivals in the inter-society competition. Many primitive societies have gone even further, using the competition for rank as a way of benefiting the community as a whole – for example, by allocating rank according to the individual's hunting ability, bravery and judgment in warfare, or success in handling the community's economic system and peacetime administration. The versatile mind of man has given the human community a tremendous advantage over every other vertebrate organization. The reigning code of honour can be moulded so that only the most profitable forms of dominance competition will be sanctioned.

Limited warfare has always offered one of the most obvious opportunities to ritualize the dominance contest in a way that profited the community. Several well-documented versions of this technique were developed by the North American Plains Indians. The ranking system practised by the Crow can be taken as fairly typical. The young Crow brave won points towards his social status by winning carefully defined honours in battle. One such honour was to lead a successful war party (horse-stealing raids and petty feuds were the normal form of battle). Another honour consisted of capturing an enemy's weapon during combat. A third was to be first to strike an enemy in the course of an engagement; and a fourth was to drive off a horse tethered in an enemy encampment. A young man who had not attained a minimum of four war honours was not regarded as fully adult. But once he had performed each of these brave deeds, he became a 'good and valiant man' and his prestige increased steadily as he added further honours to his list. The Crow band was ruled by a military elite – an administrative council of chiefs who hqd earned their rank through military triumphs and who deliberated with the councils of other bands to settle serious disputes.

The modern European may think these primitive ranking systems exotic. However, the social order of his own ancestors was very similar to that of the Crow. The competition for military honours undoubtedly played an important part in the Germanic offensive that eventually overwhelmed the Roman Empire and flooded Western Europe. The son of a Germanic chieftain was normally awarded his father's title if he was considered worthy. But first, he had to win his personal prestige through valour in battle. The young tribesman would begin his adult life by attaching himself to a mature chief of great renown, whom he would serve as a bodyguard in battle and as a courtier in peacetime. The young followers in each war leader's train competed fiercely for prestige, vying with one another for the honour of becoming second in command. The chieftains themselves competed with each other for the largest and bravest following: for them, honour lay in being surrounded by a select band of protégés. Once the fame of a succesful chieftain had spread beyond the boundaries of his tribe, his aid in battle would be solicited by foreign tribes and beleagured cantons. These would provide him with the provisions he needed for the banquets he was expected to give his men – supplementing the spoils of war. As with the American Plains Indians, the name of a revered German chieftain was often enough on its own to settle an intertribal squabble.

In Samoa, a community of greater wealth and greater size, an even more elaborate ranking system has developed. Like most Polynesian social designs, the Samoan model consists of a finely graded and ritually protected dominance hierarchy in which every individual is expected to know his place and keep in it. A man's position in the Samoan social order depends on his title. Titles are ranked according to a scale of influence originally established by the gods, with the primary division falling between sacred chiefs and talking chiefs. Essentially, the talking chief plays the part of a master of ceremonies, with different grades of talking chief officiating at public gatherings of different degrees of importance. Sacred chiefs are more awe-inspiring than the talking chiefs and carry more personal space about with them everywhere they go. They are believed to radiate a supernatural power which the gods long ago delegated to them and which will injure any untitled subordinate who fails to exhibit the proper degree of respect. The highest ranking sacred chiefs may never be touched by commoners, and they must always be addressed in a ceremonial respect language. The talking chiefs serve as spokesmen for the sacred chiefs on all public occasions, and the sacred chiefs are served sacred foods that are forbidden to ordinary men.

These chiefly titles are not normally hereditary in the same way as are such titles in caste societies. Samoan titles can only be won by means of hard work over a period of years. Although titles are owned by households and villages, and in this sense the individual owes his title to his family connections, every family possesses many more titles than could ever be filled in one generation. So everyone has almost unrestricted opportunities. However, if the young men of any particular generation are not considered title-worthy, no titles are awarded. To bestow a title on someone who could not adorn it would damage the reputation of the entire family.

The young men of Samoa compete vigorously for titles in every field open to them. Apart from the obvious economic ways of demonstrating their competence, they set themselves to learning the deportment and oratorical ability required of a chief, as well as the necessary ceremonial knowledge and skills. Intervillage warfare has for a long time been comparatively rare in Samoa but in the past, when it did break out, it presumably offered the young men numerous opportunities to gain honourable advancement. Nowadays, a more peaceful pattern applies, and titles are awarded on the basis of individual charm, integrity, judgment, and energy – generally a demonstrated capacity for leadership. As a rule, a young man rarely achieves his first title before the age of thirty. Almost all the males in the community usually get as far as the bottom rung of the title ladder by the time they are middle-aged. In this way, everybody is thoroughly involved in the system. At the same time, the awarding of titles is usually managed carefully enough to ensure that only outstanding individuals reach the topmost positions. When the highest ranking chiefs pass what they feel to be retiring age, they resign their most important titles in favour of younger men, just as the gods resigned them in favour of their ancestors, and they retain only enough of their lesser titles to keep their seats in the local council.

Generally speaking, reserved, dignified, and decisive individuals are selected for the sacred chief titles. Men marked for their eloquence and persuasiveness are picked for the talking chief titles. However, due to the important ritual part they play in public ceremonies, the highest grades of talking chief often carry a degree of prestige out of all proportion to that of the everyday flatters with whom we compared them in Chapter 4. The Samoan title system has been compared to the officer hierarchy in a modern army : individuals come and go, but the ranks and their associated character types remain unchanged. The emphasis is on the style with which a title role is executed rather than the personal idiosyncrasies of the performer. As public relations men, the talking chiefs can boost or depress the prestige of the sacred chiefs according to their own opinions and judgment. In this way, the relative rank of various titles can be adjusted to suit the abilities of the individuals in office.

Of course, no responsible talking chief would manipulate his superiors in this way except very gradually and with the utmost consideration for face. In the Samoan culture, people almost never break the rules. One of the few recognized sins among the Samoans is to talk or behave above one's rank. Insubordination is extremely rare, and the punishment for the slightest infraction, while it often may not be very painful physically, is usually extremely humiliating. A typical penalty is to make the offender sit in the sun all day with bowed head in front of the hut of the person he has offended. Anyone so foolish as to touch the clothing of a sacred chief might easily be struck down by a serious illness, and then his relatives would have to beg the chief to supply the only antidote : to touch the offender with his sacred foot.

The practice of earning prestigious, formally defined titles bring the Samoans closer to the modern status contest than the

Eskimos or the German tribesmen. Another primitive model at least as relevant to our understanding of the modern system can be found in the rank order design of the Manus.

The Manus live on the south coast of Admiralty Island, to the north of New Guinea. In this society, there are no formal titles and the socially approved personality for a male is that of an aggressive and highly efficient trader who values prestige above everything else in life. An ordinary living can be earned from fishing or canoe building. But prestige is measured in the Manus world by the amount of wealth that passes through a man's hands in ceremonial exchanges. The most important of the approved ways of exchanging ostentatious stores of wealth is by giving away exorbitant bride prices and receiving exorbitant dowry payments in return. To create opportunities for self-display, wealthy men therefore arrange the marriages of as many adopted sons and daughters as they can afford.

The extravagant gifts involved in this system often include many tons of sago. On some occasions, as many as ten thousand dogs' teeth have changed hands. Each ceremonial present is managed by an economic leader, who gives the largest part of it and who therefore gains the lion's share of the prestige. He is supported by a hierarchy of minor subscribers. Every man on the receiving side is held individually responsible for paying off his part of the debt incurred by the receipt of the gift. Since repayment may be delayed over months or years, every Manus is perpetually in debt to a chain of creditors who in turn are in debt to others. As a successful marketeer grows progressively richer, he makes increasingly extravagant exchanges of wealth with a regular exchange partner. Although this puts each one continually in debt to his partner, neither is striving to outdo the other personally. Since a man's rank is judged to be approximately equal to that of his exchange partner, each competitor is in fact encouraging his partner up the ladder of success. Each man could therefore be said to be playing against the economic community as a whole rather than against any particular individual.

Dart games, foot races, and canoe races foster the competitive way of life in Manus children from an early age. Competition in these games is fierce, and boys are encouraged to pit themselves exclusively against close rank order rivals, since only against them is victory considered to have any meaning.

Manus children are treated extremely well by adults and lead happy, irresponsible lives. But as soon as a young man marries, he becomes the most despised of adults. Margaret Mead has described how he 'must go about shy, silent, and ashamed, fishing, fetching and carrying for his financial backers'. He now owes his patron a large bride price, and he is faced with a choice between two totally different futures. On the one hand, he sees around him a handful of men who have worked hard and mastered the economic system. They have liberated themselves from their financial backers and have gone into the gift-exchange business for themselves. On the other hand, there are those who have failed to make the grade and remain totally dependent nonentities. He sees these failures being tyrannized by their younger brothers and forced to fish nightly to keep their families in food. The newly married rate as the economically unsuccessful, the 'rubbish men' of the Manus social system.

The sons of important, wealthy men in this competitive society tend to be aggressive and dominant. The sons of young and dependent men tend to be more submissive. But there are no formal hereditary class barriers in Manus society. The poorest young debtor can rise to the very top if he displays the qualities of ambition and intelligence needed to master the economic machine. By the time he reaches thirty, each male has been placed in one of the three broad categories. The lowliest consists of those men who chose not to seek honour and prestige but are content to be ordinary fishermen. One step above is a group of men who will in all likelihood continue for the rest of their lives in economic dependence and subsidiary co-operation. Most prestigious of all are the young men marked by self-assertiveness and intelligence; they are clearly cut out for future leadership. Eventually these economic marriage magnates acquire virtually dictatorial powers.

The Manus religion and ethical code both support the practical rules of the ranking system. The Manus believe that the spirits of newly dead tribesmen will visit sickness and death on those who drop out of the status race and fail to pay their debts. Such men have disregarded their fundamental duty to succeed. Under Manus mores, creditors are expected to curse debtors and to assume the right of way whenever they meet. For the ambitious young status-seeker, purgatory is not being able to curse whomever he pleases but being insulted daily by everyone.

Of course, not all primitive societies are equally devoted to the business of personal ladder climbing. Although the dominance order disposition which man appears to inherit genetically always finds some measure of expression, the emphasis varies widely from one culture to another. In some cases, the social design does very little to encourage dominance behaviour and may even go a long way towards discouraging it. In the case of the Zuni Indians of New Mexico, for example, the individual's interest in personal prestige is almost suffocated in ceremonial formalities that circumscribe every act every hour of the day. Margaret Mead has described the similarly non-competitive way of life enjoyed by the Arapesh of inland New Guinea. But what these societies gain in friendliness and tranquility they generally lose in zest and the appetite for adventure. To most modern men and women, such a non-competitive existence would seem unpalatably mild and lacking in challenge and excitement. At the other extreme, there are those societies in which the cultural pattern encourages man's competitive and hierarchical potential to the full. We might think that our own society fits this description, and it may indeed be in the upper half of the list. But it fails to qualify for first prize. Of all the primitive societies that have survived long enough to be studied by social scientists, the Kwakiutl will be remembered for possessing the classic example of a human dominance competition carried to its limits.

The Pacific coastline of northwest America, where the Kwakiutl live, is an extremely fertile area, a land of plenty. And so, with no substantial ecomonic problems to occupy their time, the Kwakiutl developed the energy-consuming device of an artificial status race to an obsessive degree. The Kwakiutl social order is characterized by an artificially created scarcity of honourable names and of the economic and religious privileges associated with them. The degree of uninhibited self-glorification that Kwakiutl society requires from its winners would be classified as megalomania in ours. In the West, the closest equivalent to an ideal Kwakiutl chieftain either conquers the known world or is quickly packed away in an asylum.

The Kwakiutl ranking system combines the main ideas behind both the Samoans and the Manus systems. The tribe is divided up into family groups, each of which possesses exclusive rights to a more or less splendid ladder of ancestral names. But no individual can assume any of the names to which he is heir unless he validates his claim with an appropriate show of acquired wealth. In theory, these names are held in trust for the oldest son of the presiding chief. In practice, there are several ways in which younger brothers can also win names. The assumption of a name must be accompanied by a *potlatch*, a ceremonial distribution of wealth which demonstrates that the individual is now sufficiently great and magnanimous to step into his ancestor's shoes. The greater the name to be assumed, the more extravagant must be the potlatch. Originally, wealth of this sort was measured mainly in cedar-bark blankets and carved wooden boxes, but in more recent years great hoards of kettles, clocks, sewing machines, and washtubs have been given away in economically useless quantities. As in Manus society, most of the wealth is presented to an established exchange rival, who loses face unless he can give back a distinctly greater gift at a later date. While the beneficiary is making the necessary economic preparations to regain his lead, he is described as being 'under the shadow' of his exchange partner's name.

When the time comes for the rival to return the potlatch, he uses the occasion as evidence that he now merits the next highest title on his own family ladder. With this lifelong objective in mind, individual rivalries are established early in a young man's life. At first, opponents may seem more like friendly co-operators than rivals, since each of them, by necessity, creates opportunities for the other to ascend the chiefly ladder. However, no Kwakiutl with any claim to self-respect can decline the challenge of a gift without admitting his subordinacy – without losing the weight of his name. To maintain his face it is absolutely necessary for him to return a more extravagant present. As the years go by and the size of the exchanges keeps increasing like a single, lifelong hand of poker, the contest for glory or utter humiliation gradually takes on an increasingly grim flavour. The potlatch always remains a grand gesture. It should not be thought of as a loan. The time soon comes when a man is only too pleased to find that his rival cannot repay him.

Every family name is believed either to have been originally obtained by an ancestor from the supernaturals after a series of challenging adventures or to contain the spirit of an ancestor who himself descended from heaven long ago. What is perhaps hardest for the modern mind to understand is the arrangement of religious beliefs through which the personalities of the Kwakiutl are attached to their names rather than to any intrinsic or real selves. Of course, this association, perhaps strange to us, greatly facilitates the psychological changes needed to accommodate the extreme mobility of Kwakiutl status-seekers. With every new rung up the ladder of sacred names, the individual sheds his old personality like a snake shedding its skin. When a chief assumes a new name during the potlatch ceremony, he feels possessed by all the greatness of the ancestor he believes he is reincarnating and he acquires a completely new ego level to match his new rank. Correspondingly, while the prize for victory in the potlatching contest is permission to enjoy a yet more glorious range of dominance feelings, a potlatch defeat completely destroys the personality along with the name. In fact, the expression 'to lose face' is more appropriate to the Kwakiutl version of the face arena than it is to the Chinese of the English. The Kwakiutl takes into himself the spirit of his ancestor by putting on a special dancing mask which is handed down from generation to generation. The chief who loses face loses the right to wear his mask and therefore loses the glorious spirit with whom he identified.

Every individual born into Kwakiutl society is trained to this competitive and extremely hierarchical way of life from early childhood. A chief normally encourages his firstborn son to throw stones at people who have no names – this helps him learn at an early age the proper attitude towards his inferiors. When he is born, a baby is given a name which refers only to his place of birth. As soon as the time comes for him to assume a name of greater importance, the elders of his family give him property to distribute to his relatives. These gifts are returned promptly with excessive interest, and this provides the young chiefling with his first stock of wealth. When enough small exchanges have taken place to build this stock up to a respectable sum, the young man is ready for his first potlatch. During the ceremony, his father confers on him one of the lower ranking family names and from then on he is considered a full-fledged member of the tribe. With his first potlatch, he launches himself irrevocably on the fame-obsessed career which the gods and the ancestors of the Kwakiutl have seen fit to bequeath to their descendants.

An institution as significant as the potlatch ceremony is certain to be reflected in all other aspects of the cultural pattern. As in Manus society, Kwakiutl marriages are accompanied by ostentatious exchanges, partly because a wife brings with her certain rights to her family's names. These exchanges give additional opportunities for glorifying oneself and for insulting rivals. Marriages that are not accompanied by the proper show of wealth are no more marriages than were the pair-bonds in Christian Europe which were not accompanied by the appropriate rites. The Kwakiutl refer to such arrangements as 'sticking together like dogs'. Although there is some evidence to suggest a tendency towards a hereditary class system among the Kwakiutl, this stage has never been reached. The elder son gets nearly all the promotion, and he alone inherits the right to the family's most glorious names, but a younger son of great ability can always find a way around that obstacle. He can move off and join his mother's family, where he might be eligible for some of her ancestral names. Or he may become a shaman and climb up a second potlatch pyramid within the religio-magical sector of the society, which more or less parallels the secular hierarchy. In some cases, it is possible to murder a man and thereby replace or consume him – name and privileges included.

In one way or another, everybody who is anybody in Kwakiutl society is involved in the ranking contest. The women and children are absorbed into the system as subsidiary helpers, and no one can imagine any other way of calculating real social worth. The small man who handles blankets in lots of five or ten is as deeply committed to this view of life as is the big man who counts his blankets in thousands. The only difference between them is that the small man experiences pride and shame in smaller quantities. The prime objective in life is not simply to gain wealth but to eliminate rivals completely by outgiving them. It is this unrestrained competition which forces the Kwakiutl to extremes of dominance feeling and behaviour which neither the Samoans nor the Manus reach. As we mentioned earlier, the psychiatrist John Scott Price believes that the elation and depression found in many psychiatric patients are merely the extremes on a prescribed scale of emotions which equip man for hierarchical living, and he has suggested testing his theories by examining human behaiour in an environment especially structured to induce competition. As far as the natural laboratory provided by the Kwakiutl is concerned, we must conclude that Price's hypothesis is borne out. In the Kwakiutl society, types of behaviour which the Western world would classify as manic elation and chronic depression fall within the normal range of responses.

The rising champions of Kwakiutl society are totally dedicated to 'crushing their rivals with property'. Victory is therefore accompanied by a tremendous sense of elation. Wallowing in self-glorification, the victor may boast that he is going to pull mountains to pieces to use the stones for his fire. Much as we might dress in a particular style of clothing, the ideal Kwakiutl man dresses himself in a personality to match such ancestral names as: Pillar of Heaven, River of Wealth, The Great One Always Alone in the World, Giving away Blankets while Walking, Giving Potlatch Everywhere, About Whose Property People Talk, Creating Trouble All Around, Getting Too Great.

If Price's hypothesis is correct, we would expect this degree of elation in the winners to be balanced by an approximately equivalent degree of depression in the losers. If a chief is unable to return the potlatch expected of him, his name is 'broken'. Since his dominance feelings depend on his name, he feels completely 'flattened'. There are now only two courses open to him. He can set off on an extremely dangerous headhunting expedition which holds little chance of survival but does provide at least some chance of regaining face. Or he can finally hide his face by committing suicide, a comparatively common event among the Kwakiutl. The individual stakes everything on a grandiose picture of himself. The continuing sense of personal glory is what life is all about, and life without it is unbearable. Often the suicide is a passive, automatic act. The defeated individual simply dies of shame: 'He wasn't sick at all – he just dropped down. The other one went to Frazer River that Summer, and he also died there without being sick – just dropped down dead'.

The Modern Success Story

These examples of primitive ranking systems illustrate how human communities living under widely different conditions have resorted to an equally wide variety of techniques for establishing their dominance orders. But no matter how strange and specialized the rank-deciding machinery may be, it is never so alien that we cannot comprehend the logic of the contest. Despite the variety, there appears to be a limited range of possibilities within which even the most imaginative design must remain.

Stealing another man's wife and then engaging in a public confrontation may not be a method we would want to choose ourselves, but we have no difficulty in understanding the way in which prestige can be won and lost on this basis. The technique of defining the rank order by a point for point list of honourable achievements, as did the Crow Indians, has developed time and time again in different cultural contexts. This principle was central to the knight-errant tradition of medieval Europe (a refinement of the old Germanic ranking system), and a similar approach to war honours developed among fighter pilots in both the recent world wars. The way in which the Manus champion uses ostentatious marriage ceremonies to gain and display status is comparable with the European tradition, in which the head of the bride's family invests in an expensive and showy wedding reception – mainly for the sake of gaining prestige for himself, for the married couple, and for the associated friends and relatives. Even the Kwakiutl method of climbing the rank order ladder, while it may seem exotic, is far from incomprehensible. Anthropologists have compared the system of the potlatch to the way in which modern citizens may gain and lose face through the ritual exchange of dinners and entertainments, Christmas and birthday presents.

Perhaps the most important feature that all these ranking systems share is the broad type of personality that gets to the top. Whatever the form of the competition, the winners will always be found among the most assertive members of the community – the men who have the most courage and determination, who project mana, who display most clearly the characteristics typical of all high-dominance primates. The ideal American Plains Indian brave has usually been a courageous and intelligent warrior who is also a persuasive speech-maker. The Manus man destined to reach the top is an assertive and hard-working trader with the ability to plan and to arrive at shrewd commercial judgments and with some skill in public speaking. In Samoa, emphasis is placed on the title an individual carries rather than on the person himself. However, the Samoan title system channels into itself the potentially dominant and energetic young men, and Samoans carrying the higher titles are usually outstanding individuals. Although the great names of the Kwakiutl are hereditary, the property necessary for validating a name must be gained by energetic and skilful manipulation. The individual who inherits little opportunity for acquiring great names can get around this problem in several ways. Moreover, the prestige of a Kwakiutl chief does not depend solely on the formal grandeur of his name. He is also judged according to the zeal with which he displays his pride at a potlatch.

Apparently, any ranking system that attempted to select individuals on a basis totally unrelated to these fundamental aspects of dominance would find it difficult, if not impossible, to establish a credible pattern of authority. The primitive ranking system has had to select the age-old qualities involved in primate dominance just as surely as the hereditary class system depended on selectively encouraging these qualities in the aristocratic mind. Although the rules of the game have now changed in a great many ways, these qualities are still found to mark the man who rises to the top of the modern business pyramid.

According to a recent review of leadership traits in American business, the number one secret of executive success is 'the ability to maintain a high level of thrust'. Successful competitors in the new commercial arena are described as men who explode with energy even in leisure-time activities. As with the Manus marriage magnate, the personality pattern of the top-notch American executive is widely regarded as a product of the individual's determination not to get left behind in the competition. Many a modern 'tiger of industry' would no doubt agree with his Kwakiutl counterpart that the minute-by-minute confirmation of an exalted ego level is what life is about. Certainly his ideological commitment to success is striking. When he is not engaged in outstripping all standards of comparison, he supposedly grows uneasy and paces up and down the deep pile of the chief executive carpet. It is generally agreed that the essential ingredients for a self-made millionaire are courage and vision and an ability to roll with the punches.

None of the primitive earned-rank systems we have been describing were able to contain the number of individuals the hereditary class system could bind together. But now the modern industrial society has replaced its aristocratic predecessor in still larger communities with the most elaborate earned-rank system man has ever known. Already this new technique has become vastly more complicated than anyone could have envisaged as little as a century ago. The ranking job of the old primate pseudo-fight has been taken over by more and more sophisticated ranking systems until we have now arrived at a complex set of interrelated competitions that all contribute to a single gigantic status contest.

The modern industrial ranking system has replaced the hereditary class system because it makes fuller use of a community's total supply of manpower and ambition. In particular, it avoids the one or two outstanding technical faults in the hereditary class technique which have repeatedly brought that system to a collapse. Time and time again, increasingly rigid class barriers became so impenetrable that not enough energy and intelligence could climb up through them to keep the community competently administered. Often the ambitious individuals thus frustrated were not merely wasted but turned into virulent enemies of the state, becoming bandits or pirates. Under the new rules, these absolute barriers have now been lifted. Every young man is encouraged to aim high. Not only does this ensure a maximum of effort along the socially approved channels, it also means that the top positions will eventually be filled by approximately the ablest men possible. They may seem relaxed and imperturbable once they have reached the top, but they will have been the most ambitious and hardest working youngsters of their generation.

The Importance of Being Rich

The written laws of the courtroom and the informal codes of polite and honourable social conduct together make up an intricate network of rules within which the modern ranking system operates. Successful competitors are awarded titles such as Minister of Housing, Managing Director of IBM, or President of the State Bank. As a rule, these titles can only be won through achievements that are judged to be of service to the community. Depending on which door he chooses, the young competitor may one day become an executive director, a professor of agricultural chemistry, a judge, or a city councillor – all equivalent, in a sense, to the Samoan sacred chiefs. The talking chiefs have their counterparts in television interviewers, film directors, and the administrators of the communications industry – who are all able to boost or depress the status of a particular sacred title or titleholder.

The wealth philosophy of the Manus and the Kwakiutl also has its counterpart in modern industrial society. Competitors in the modern status contest can also earn honour and prestige by accumulating points in the form of money. A century ago in Europe, the defenders of the hereditary class system were still very reluctant to give any dominance value to earned wealth. The aristocrat took it for granted that wealth should properly be inherited in proportion to the brilliance of the ancestral title it had to support. But now earned wealth has come to play a central part in the competition for prestige throughout the so-called capitalist or free-enterprise societies. Every pound, franc, mark, yen, or dollar counts as a small but exactly standardized unit of social priority. The man who can pay the price gains possession of the commodity. The man who can pay the wage gains command of the servant. The use of money as a means of allocating formal priorities makes it possible to measure out more degrees of rank than any other method known. It allows contestants to be rewarded pro rata for units of achievement that are not distinct enough in themselves to merit a title. It makes it possible for young members of the community to enjoy a measure of prestige prior to earning their titles and so gives them an early taste of the rewards they will get for striving hard in competitive service to the community.

Many people still fear that a money-based rank order must inevitably result in the exploitation of the many by the few. Throughout the 19th century, the spectre of a new and more brutal capitalist aristocracy loomed over the industrial world. But this prophetic vision had little to do with the basic principle of rank by money points. The political outcome depends on the rules which govern the way that money points are awarded and in particular on whether they can be inherited. The comparatively crude social and economic rules that prevailed a hundred years ago seemed to many people to be pushing humanity inevitably towards a society where masses of human tools would be exploited by a small hereditary class of industrial proprietors. Since then many changes in the rules have come about which show that this early premonition was not justified.

If all consumable goods and items of economic value can be bought directly with status points, then every member of the community can enjoy the success he achieves in a wide variety of optional ways. He can arrange to spend his dominance exactly how and when he chooses. In cultures where prestige is distributed in the form of titles, the winner has far less control over the ways in which he is allowed to enjoy success, and his reward must consist more completely in being treated to displays of deference. This means that, to a much greater extent, one man's success must involve another man's subordination. In this sense, the principle of rank by money points offers greater personal freedom throughout the community than could ever be achieved by a system based on titles alone.

A ranking system based on money points gives every individual the widest possible choice of whom and when to obey. This is not to say that titles have no use in a money-oriented society. They can have a long list of special obligations attached to them, and they involve a personal commitment to an honourable code of conduct – this makes it possible to keep a tight control on the ways very high-ranking individuals exercise their prestige. It is far more difficult to control the power of men whose prestige has been accumulated in the form of money alone. Nevertheless, the part played by money is now becoming so important that titles are increasingly meaningless unless they are accompanied by an appropriate store of wealth. The dominant social role has always involved a degree of display and largesse, and both of these cost money. Consequently, titles which were once held sacred but which are now worn by poor men are coming to be seen as empty honours. Few senior titleholders are now expected to get by without an expense and entertainment account. On the other hand, the chiefly title of millionaire is awarded automatically and indiscriminately as soon as an individual has accumulated the required quota of points.

Whenever a primitive society suddenly grew so large that it began to separate into hereditary classes, the aristocratic sub-group depended for its survival on cornering the lion's share of the community's wealth. If this wealth took the form of tribute from subjugated neighbour states, the ruling class had to legitimize some system of keeping the tribute to itself. In cultures in which wealth came mainly from the land, the aristocrats owned the land. With the industrial revolution and the upward striving of a new class of commercial administrators, the European aristocrat was faced with the problem of retaining control over the many new and changing sources of wealth. Although this was not a totally new problem, no other hereditary class system had met it in such a troublesome form before. The most outstanding chieftains of the rising class were invited to join the lower ranks of the aristocracy provided they submitted to its traditional value system and brought with them their share of control in the new industrial ecomony. However, the mass of lowborn but ambitious and capable individuals spawned by this new technology eventually proved too powerful to be contained. Aristocratic defenders of the old order could easily keep control of the distribution of titles, but it was impossible to keep track of the rapidly multiplying and ever-changing methods of making money. Both titles and money points now play important parts in the modern earned-rank system, but money was the horse that the aristocrat defenders could not break to the saddle. Accordingly, we find that the rise of the new earned-rank system paralleled the growth of commercial power in Europe. The measures adopted by the aristocratic defenders of the old hereditary class system to keep their subordinate subgroups submissive and intact are as interesting as the devious ways in which the meritocratic principle finally overcame every obstacle put in its path. Together they make up the exciting story of how the modern industrial ranking system eventually came to power – an important chapter in the history of the human dominance order.

The victory of the new system was not won easily. To preserve their power and the hereditary laws and values that supported it, the aristocratic classes tried every means of diverting the energies of their subordinates into harmless or advantageous channels. As long as they held the reins, they were free to change the rules to suit themselves. The most effective method of preserving their dominance was to persuade the lower classes to seek legitimate prestige in ways that helped the aristocrat. Ambitious commoners were given minor privileges in reward for services to the status quo. They were encouraged to become glorious warriors and even second-class military administrators. They were permitted to become minor bureaucratic officials with enough privileges to give them a stake in preserving the system from collapse. A small proportion of excellent low-caste manpower could usually be married to the aristocratic cause, and a small number of completely new memberships could be carefully rationed out along the lines of a life peerage.

On the other side of the scale, the aristocratic classes were always poorly co-ordinated in their methods of defence. Although every law, every custom, every detail of the religious trestle table which upheld the sanctity of the cultural pattern was in the control of the aristocrats, they were greatly restricted by their own lack of efficient co-operation and by their almost universal ignorance of what was happening. They simply could not stand outside the situation, as we do today, and look down on the scene to get a clear view of events.

Until the emergence of modern industrial society, the conservative forces backing the hereditary principle were able to beat off repeated charges from the earned-rank camp. The defensive measures taken by the ruling class in the Aztec Empire to keep commercial upstarts in their proper place are typical of the ways that blue-blooded authority has usually been preserved. Successful merchants who made a display of their new riches were put to death by imperial command, and their possessions were then distributed in what seemed the only conceivably moral way – they were given to the hereditary administrators of their districts and to the few self-made military commanders who had to be rewarded for their loyalty. According to the Spaniards who arrived in Mexico in 1519, the merchants living under Aztec rule were forced to wear worn-out cloaks and to walk with their eyes lowered to the ground. But behind the scenes they were steadily gaining in power, and by the time of the conquest the aristocrats were beginning to attend their feasts and accept their presents. What would have been the end result of this process can only be guessed at, but the Spaniards found that already highly placed dignitaries were finding it profitable to marry merchants' daughters, at least as secondary wives.

Identical patterns have been repeated time and again in the large hereditary class systems of Europe and Asia. The fact that these separate social movements developed independently along such closely parallel lines suggests that the rise of the new earned-rank system was as inevitable as had been the emergence of the older hereditary class system. The way in which the commercial classes repeatedly pushed for authority indicates that the efforts made to check the slow displacement of hereditary rank were eventually doomed to failure. In the end, the more efficient ranking method had to win; the patterns that could be seen developing in the Aztec Empire eventually triumphed in the European arena.

The aristocrats in Europe were forced into just the same mixture of simple defences and short-sighted compromises to keep the earned-rank ethic in check. Few if any aristocrats ever recognized the enemy. They thought they were dealing with people, not with an abstract social design. To the aristocrat, there seemed to be only a small number of lowborn trouble-makers who worked like water rats and cheated on the rules. We have already noted how the wives of rich medieval merchants were restrained from wearing extravagant clothes that displayed their husbands' wealth. At a later stage, impoverished French noblemen began to mix freely with wealthy merchants and tax farmers and to marry their daughters for the sake of the dowry. But the industrial revolution opened up so many new paths to money power that the system finally burst the banks within which the hereditary forces had tried to contain it. The new technology brought such complex economic patterns in its wake that the hereditary tradition could no longer supply sufficient administrative skill to govern the community. The newly emerging industrial society was forced to accept the fact that to award rank on the basis of earned points produced a much more efficient system.

The worldwide pattern of aristocratic hostility towards wealthy merchants testifies to the fundamental relationship between wealth and dominance that finally put power into the merchant's hands. Eventually, the European Renaissance saw the development of international trade leagues webbing together hundreds of towns and villages. The emergence of comparatively democratic towns and city-states limited the aristocrat's ability to keep the merchant under his thumb. City life allowed the new earned-rank system to get a firm grip and, at last, enough breathing space to formulate its own book of rules. Within two generations, Italian bankers had produced the first written code of commercial laws and were underwriting the politics of Europe. For as long as the trump cards remained in the aristocrat's hand, he had been able to hang the merchant and steal his purse with the blessing of the Almighty Judge. But once the merchant was over the hill, the whole ethical system turned to favour a rank order based on earned points. The hereditary cause was lost. Behind the merchant marched an invincible army of soberly dressed death-duty collectors, camouflaged technocrats, poor-boy presidents and self-made multi-millionaires.

The industrialization of eighteenth- and nineteenth-century England rewarded entrepreneurial competence with such a degree of de facto power that it was impossible to resist the claim of the commercial class to formal authority. As far as possible, this new social assertiveness was diverted into the building of an empire and the conquering of foreign tribes. This delayed takeover by the new ranking system sufficiently for the aristocrat to go on treating money as a mere provider, a convenient economic unit for the exercise of his natural privilege. He could still refuse to see it as a legitimate system of earned points bearing any relevance to rank in the garden-party situation. But the professional classes clinging to the skirts of the hereditary elite and imitating their values in return for a small share of their prestige had more to gain and less to lose. They were more vulnerable to the persuasive moral arguments that the new rules brought along with them.

Religion and the Rank Order

Written and unwritten laws define the rules of the new status contest and control the behaviour of all individuals who seek generally accredited rank. Dominance within this system is for the most part achieved by winning points and titles. But all these features of the ranking system cannot work together effectively unless every member of the community accepts their unique legitimacy. In the Western world, the hereditary class system is in its final stages of decay because an ever-increasing body of people refuses to acknowledge that there is anything sacred about its underlying precepts. Unless all members of the Eskimo community acknowledge the validity of a song contest defeat, the ritual will have failed to do its job. The various ways in which primitive societies induce their members to accept unquestioningly their particular set of ranking rules throw light on the way modern society ensures that its members view the rules of the new status contest as the only possible ones.

By defining the arena within which ambitious individuals must confine their status contests, society harnesses the most explosive source of energy in a human community. But at least half the job is to ensure that everybody abides by the rules. The different techniques that various societies have developed to achieve this have always made use of man's innate emotional ability to subordinate himself to something he perceives as a superior power. In a primitive society, the rules of the prevailing ranking system express themselves in legends, myths, taboo, and religion. They take their authority from gods and heroes whose legendary adventures illustrate that society's vision of the ideal man.

In a primitive society, the ambitious young man normally makes no attempt to better his elders' achievements. He generally accepts without question the superiority of all the members of his father's generation, and his main concern is simply to prove himself worthy of his ancestors. The seniors of the community serve as living models to the young. Their judgment is not to be questioned and the generation gap is never crossed. This simple conservative pattern has had a socially useful side effect. Each young man usually feels such a deep respect for his elders that the champions of each generation are progressively heroized by every succeeding one. This provides an evolving social design with a continually updated stream of legendary characters who can be ostentatiously praised for exemplifying those ranking criteria that are most in need of public-relations support.

Religious beliefs and legendary sagas support individual dominance relationships and help to standardize the social attitudes of a whole community. They ensure that all the effort exerted by young status-seekers is channelled in an approved and orderly way. At the same time, they increase the self-assurance of those with high rank by guaranteeing their authority. In other words, the community's supporting system of religious beliefs helps each individual to make whatever psychological adjustments are necessary to accept his position in the prevailing dominance order.

The Kwakiutl offer a particularly clear example of this relationship between religion and rank. Not surprisingly, the Kwakiutl religion is inextricably involved with the contest for prestige. Contact with the supernatural is restricted by privileges which are inherited through the family and which have to be validated by the potlatch ceremony. A similar connection between rank and religion can be seen in the Kwakiutl attitude towards good luck. To the primitive mind, nothing ever happens by accident, and for the Kwakiutl a piece of good fortune is seen as a gift from the gods. An outstanding run of luck, at gambling, for example, adds to the individual's prestige, just as a man who receives ten blankets from a magnanimous chief is thereby shown to be of higher rank than a man who is given only five. Unless he knew what sort of behaviour the Kwakiutl expect of their ideal chieftains, a modern observer would find it difficult to understand Kwakiutl gods. A Kwakiutl god who fails to distribute good fortune among his people is evaluated in the same way as a chief with a big name who fails to give the magnanimous potlatch expected of him. An early Christian traveller among the Kwakiutl reported: 'When calamities are prolonged or thicken, they get enraged against God and vent their anger against him, raising their eyes and hands in savage anger to heaven, stamping their feet on the ground and repeating "You are a great Slave." It is their greatest term of reproach.'

The myths and religious beliefs of medieval Europe also served the prevailing ranking system. In this case, a hereditary class system was supported by the formulae of the Christian church and the moral messages contained in numerous semi-religious legends and folktales. Church theorists taught that a single Almighty Father God had shaped the universe into a strict hierarchical scale that ranged from himself at the top to inanimate stones at the bottom. Nothing in this 'chain of being' could hope to move up a rung in the ladder by any means whatsoever. One step below the magic overlord ranked the angels, neatly arranged into subsidiary orders among themselves. Between the angels and the animals came man, graded downwards from kings to commoners. If heaven was thus ranked by divine command, it was obvious that the world of men should obey the same logic. The feudal aristocrat who wielded worldly power was unlikely to disagree. The Father God clearly wanted his mortal world to be ruled by hereditary princes. He had set the magical precedent himself.

When the medieval peasant attended church, he could see for himself that the priests must have been appointed by the Father God. Otherwise, the god would never have allowed them to handle the affairs of his sacred house. Moreover, they were the only men who could speak the ancient and magical tongue in which he had originally voiced the sacred rules. Usually the local aristocrats sat in raised and ornamented pews, either in the front or to one side of the congregation. From the peasant's point of view, they must have seemed more like overseers than co-worshippers. At least once a week the feudal community would get together in a ceremony of shared veneration to reaffirm their rank order relationships in the humbling presence of their Almighty Maker. The rich man in his castle, the poor man at his gate – he had made them high and lowly, he had ordered their estate. At every possible point, the religion of the era was intertwined with the hereditary class system that actually ran the show. A reflection of this close collaboration between church and state survives in the British national anthem. At the close of most formal occasions, hereditary subordinates traditionally sing to their spiritual father to make their hereditary overlord victorious, happy, and glorious, and to permit him to reign over them for as long as possible.

The rise of the modern ranking system coincided with the slow disintegration of the rank order ideology the medieval church had helped to maintain. Originally, the god's appointed custodians of spiritual health were unalterably opposed to the emerging acquisitive philosophy of the lower orders and to the obviously dangerous ranking system that accompanied it. God had not placed the rich man in his castle arbitrarily. The job of the church was to make it clear that he wanted things to stay as they were, and under his heavenly licence it enforced the rules he had seen fit to prescribe. Worldly status-striving was denounced as a sinful vanity. The acquisitive appetite was seen as the work of the devil. If John the cartwright wished to accumulate points, he was best advised to collect the sort that would count in the next world. Generally speaking, this policy was compatible with the practical conditions of the day. Each man's niche in the class ladder was his whole world. He accepted the rank he was allotted and believed that the people born above him were, in fact, more worthy than he was. A medieval peasant or craftsman simply would not have comprehended the question, 'What would you do if you were suddenly made an aristocrat?' It would have been like asking a low-caste South African farm worker what he would do if he were suddenly transformed into a white man. In neither case could the subordinate realistically conceive himself to be in such a position.

In time, the new ranking system began to push through in the European towns. But first it had to reshuffle the religious beliefs that supported the old system it was destined to replace. A new ethic had to be legitimized in the minds of a mass of superstitious people. The traumatic upheaval of the Reformation saw the doctrines of the medieval church revised, and a new interpretation of the ranking rules swept across half of Europe. The rising middle class brought its accumulation of incontestable points to the altar as well as to parliament. After counting the coins, God changed his mind, and, with the aid of several rancorous clerics, rewrote his sacred rule book for the bourgeoisie. With a sweep of the Grand Designer's editing pencil, individual toil and determination became legitimate grounds for claiming dominance in the earthbound society of men.

High finance had once been considered a despicable practice carried on largely by the Jew who had rejected Christ. Now it became a commendable profession for honest, God-fearing citizens. Gradually, the accumulated nest egg came to be seen as one of the ways in which the Almighty showed his favour; the Puritan succeeded in sanctifying his money. It was demeaning to spend capital to satisfy the flesh; he who did this cancelled his heavenly trading licence. But as long as these worldly riches were accumulated in the name of God's greater glory on Earth, the pursuit of wealth became a sacred duty. The medieval church had taught that the highest of all gods presided over a universal hereditary class system. The Protestant church now taught that a slightly reinterpreted God had deliberately designed the unequal distribution of wealth. Poverty was a sign of slothfulness. It showed a lack of the new divine attributes – diligence and frugality. God did not extend his grace to those who remained poor. Either they had failed to use their talents or they were damned by predestination. Whichever the case, the reasons behind their failure were not available for examination. The divine will pursued divine ends unfathomable to man.

Within half a century, the Reformation greatly altered the European's attitude to social worth. But it did not complete the religious revolution associated with the new ranking system at one blow. This first revision of the moral substructure was only an early link in the chain of ideological convulsions. It took more than two generations of heretics to turn a whole religion inside out. The Protestant's early success in sanctifying his profits marked only the first step in the spiritual take-over of the new system. It was not enough merely to establish that toil was worthy of reward. The whole magical framework had to be rearranged around the idea of toil, so that earned rank could become the central pivot of the new religion. In the centuries following the reformation, successive waves of ideological revision have gradually strengthened the authority of the earned-rank ethic at the expense of its medieval counterpart.

The revolution that has already taken place in the Western world's ranking ideology is evident when we compare the training of a medieval child to that of his modern counterpart. The flag of equal opportunity has now been flying over industrial city life for nearly two centuries. One result is that the child's parents are no longer presented to him as models of perfect behaviour; if they were, it would unjustly limit his social aspiration. The central implication of the compulsory education system is that parents cannot be automatically considered adequate teachers. Today's child is no longer concerned with proving himself worthy of his father. Only by improving on his father's success can he justify in his own mind the claim to have done anything better than break even. The modern child is born into a world where almost the only people to be respected are men and women possessing individually earned wealth and individually earned titles. There is less reason to fear these new overlords, but respect still comes from the heart; as exemplified by the feeling that 'to have gotten to where he's gotten to, he must be good'. Life is explicitly presented to the child as a free-for-all in which he starts out being just as good as the next man.

Equality before the law and the still more general dogma that all men are equal are both key struts within the modern ideological structure. The minimum degree of face which all individuals are now guaranteed derives its justification from these principles. However, the idea of social equality does not mean that an individual cannot earn additional respect over and above the sacred minimum. The equality of all men refers as much to an equal right to self-improvement. The successful individual has a legitimate claim to a greater than ordinary degree of face as long as his behaviour is consistent with the conventional prestige system.

Industrial Serfs and Sacred Chiefs

The new earned-rank system has already proved so successful that a number of slightly different versions of the basic design are now jockeying for the leading position: Western societies emphasize the usefulness of money-points rather than titles. Marxist societies have inherited the distrust of money as a measure of prestige and rely more heavily on titles. In the long run the most successful designs will be those in which rank is awarded on a scale that suits the competitive requirements of the community. At the same time, the right to survive and expand will presumably fall to those social designs which most cleverly adapt themselves to the needs of the individual rather than to those which depend on suppressing unwanted elements of genetically prescribed human nature.

For the present, the Western versions of the industrial dominance order probably involve the most complex and sophisticated ranking system that man has ever developed. However, at the individual level, we remain emotionally committed to the primitive laws of the ritual pseudo-fight. A primitive Samoan or Manus tribesman would find many things to astonish him in the competitive rules of twentieth-century America. But he would immediately recognize the essential ingredients of space-age prestige. All around him he would see rank order pyramids whose detailed structures baffled him completely. On the other hand, he would easily understand that these pyramids were there to be climbed by ambitious young men until the whole community had been ordered into a system of sacred chiefs, minor functionaries, salary earners, and industrial serfs.

For the present, the comparative rating of responsible authorities and influential celebrities is still uncertain. The dust of rapid change has yet to settle. Among the confused are the presidents and prime ministers of these new industrial nations. The prevailing political designs require them to win the direct personal support of a giant television-watching community, and this forces them to tiptoe uncertainly between the reserve traditionally appropriate to authorities and the opportunism of applause-conscious celebrities. However, despite the loose ends, the main features of the new social pattern are clearly visible. Rigid caste divisions have given way to a continuous social scale on which each individual may rise and fall. Nevertheless, certain broad rank order categories can easily be distinguished. Like the low-ranking Manus fishermen, the serfs of the industrial dominance order have resigned themselves to a way of life completely devoid of prestige. But by far the greater part of the population falls into a category we could loosely call the middle ranks. As a rule, they have some money to spend on luxuries but they have no titles and seldom anticipate winning any. Instead, they compete with one another in minor displays of wealth. They strain their budgets to the limit in pursuit of small-scale dominance symbols such as fashionable clothing and multipoint motor cars – objects which the high-ranking metropolitan titleholder normally takes for granted.

A few successful competitors from within this group may accumulate a substantial stock of points and begin to fraternize with titleholders in the hope of sanctifying their assets. However, these are the exceptions. The majority accept their sub-title status and find excitement in the adventures of their betters as reported by newspapers, magazines, and television. For the most part, their interest in the glamourous world of title-holders and title seekers remains passive. The vicarious excitement of other people's triumphs and failures is admittedly living secondhand, but it remains more attractive than working hard in off hours towards additional points or titles. Having accepted that the world of bright lights and beautiful people is not for him, the subordinate allows his dreams and his realistic ambitions to drift into two separate compartments rather than combine them in a practicable life-long plan of action.

Many of the individuals in this group may have started out intent on winning one of the most prominent titles in their respective occupational hierarchies. But with each rung up the ladder, the competition gets stiffer. Even if the contestant has the necessary intelligence and the capacity to work hard, he may soon find that he lacks the self-confidence to manage the increasingly important decisions required of him and the increasingly assertive people with whom he has to deal. His morale is sapped by constant anxiety. Spells of depression lead to a decline in performance, which in turn leads to further anxiety. His superiors are forced to conclude that it would be unwise to promote him further. His colleagues will describe him as having 'topped out'. As in any other dominance hierarchy, it appears that the individual can seldom maintain a position higher than the one for which his dominance feelings qualify him.

The lower the individual stands in this modern earned-rank dominance order, the less skill and comprehension he displays concerning the methods of accumulating power. Not only does the serf makes no attempt to win a title but he has little ability to handle points. He has no respect for money. As we move higher up into the middle ranks, an increasing number of individuals stay solvent and make use of standard techniques for lending points to the economic machine at small but guaranteed rates of interest. These two groups account for nearly the whole of the population numerically, but, as in Manus society, there is that small proportion of youngsters born in the stables who work hard and well for a lifetime and eventually climb to the top. (Generally speaking, the pretender to titles must cultivate much the same sort of grace and charm and ceremonial savoir-faire that counted in old Samoa. This is what distinguishes him from the dishonourable competitor who simply pushes and pays, using his money unscrupulously to domineer where he fails to dominate.) As the dedicated title seeker climbs the chiefly ladder, he learns more adventurous ways of multiplying his points. Fixed rates of interest and fixed salaries help to set up the table on which the really exciting cards are dealt. Subsidiary co-operation is eventually left behind for others to make the best of it, and the challenger enters the centre ring for the most psychologically exacting contest ever invented.

In a modern industrial society, the dominant man possesses both wealth and titles. Accordingly, his rank order honours bring him much the same priorities and privileges that an aristocratic lineage would have secured him in a hereditary class society. Perhaps the most obvious aspect of the dominant man's continuing legacy is the cluster of subordinate functionaries forever at his side. We might compare his position to that of a nobleman, accompanied everywhere by personal retainers. Since the modern legal system ensures that all subordinates serve voluntarily, they must be well treated. This helps to reduce any pangs of egalitarian conscience the dominant man might otherwise feel as he enjoys the services of chauffeurs, secretaries, press attachés and legal advisors, butlers and concubines. All these subordinates can demand an increasingly high price for their services, but they feel obliged to do their jobs proportionately well.

In primitive societies throughout the world, the most honourable prestige contests take the form of competitive largesse. We have seen how the big men in Manus and Kwakiutl communities validate their claims to rank with displays of magnanimity when they meet their rivals in the gift-giving contest. Players who fail to conduct this ritual exchange with the required extravagance and regard for etiquette gain a reputation for being 'slow' or 'hard' in the potlatch. A particularly mean man may be denounced for conducting his potlatches in the same spirit that he barters pigs. In a similar way, the dominant man in modern society must support his claim to face by taking part in the ritual exchange of extravagant entertainments. His greater resources of wealth raise him above the middle-ranker's preoccupation with mass-produced status symbols. Instead of spending extravagantly on clothes and cars in an effort to keep up with the Joneses, the big man in the industrial dominance order throws charity balls and Mediterranean cruises to keep up with his exchange rivals. The wealthier he is, the more splendid his potlatches can be and the more select and celebrated his acknowledged competition.

The behaviour patterns associated with dominance and deference are deeply inscribed on man's inherited circuitry, and it does not matter greatly to the winners of the modern status contest whether a subordinate is paid for his deference in sophisticated money points or volunteers it out of some more primitive source of respect. Although widespread wealth and legal protection have eliminated some of the most unpleasant emotional pressures subordination once implied, all the less painful parts of the deferent syndrome remain the same. The losers of the Manus status race resign themselves to a monotonous hand-to-mouth existence forever under the shame of debt. The wealthy champions dominate the community and their personal judgment is virtually law. The comparison with the modern system is unmistakable. The new morality would never allow a child to be born under the burden of debt, but a steadily increasing number of lower ranking community members now spend much of their adult lives in the red. In practice, they can afford luxuries that would astonish the most extravagant of old world princes, but the shadow of a negative bank balance is certain to have a depressing effect on the individual's social assertiveness in a society which admires wealth so highly. Clearly this helps the employee to adjust his level of dominance feelings to suit the subordinate role required of him.

The self-made modern chieftain may or may not believe himself to be morally superior to his paid lackeys. However, the self-assurance he needed to win his honours can only be reinforced by the fact that he is now surrounded by subordinates eager to be of service. The fact of his success will bring him mana – that ability to command attention. The heartfelt deference of his magically measured inferiors inevitably encourages in him a dominant state of mind. The modern industrial ranking system views everyone with increasing benevolence, and already the small man is assured of an unprecedented degree of face. For the present, however, his personal values and his social outlook continue to differ vastly from those enjoyed by his new chieftains. Characteristically, each individual knows only his own range of dominance feelings, in this social design as in any other. He still tends to imagine that this is the complete spectrum of possibilities. In fact, he usually experiences only a small section of the total range of dominance feelings experienced throughout the community. The view from the basement is psychologically a million miles away from the view out of the wide window at the top of the building. What may seem to one man a purposeless rat race is another's compelling adventure.

NOTES AND BIBLIOGRAPHY

[Note: Figures beside notes refer to related text pages.]

NOTES TO CHAPTER I

7. Research into mechanics of human communication: Michael Argyle et al., 'The Communication of Inferior and Superior Attitudes by Verbal and Non-Verbal Signals,' *British Journal of Social and Clinical Psychology* 9 (1970): 222.

7. Three dominance categories: this topic is expanded in Chapter Two (see Chapter 2, 30–31).

8–9. Social scientists incorporating ethological perspective: L. Tiger and R. Fox, 'The Zoological Perspective in Social Science,' *Man* 1, no. 1 (March 1966): 75. See also articles by G. Gaylord Simpson and Anne Roe, Harry F. Harlow, Robert H. Knapp, John W. Riley, in *The Behavioral Sciences Today*, ed. Bernard Berelson (New York: Harper and Row, 1963).

9–10. Chicken run pecking order: T. Schjelderup-Ebbe, 'Social Behavior of Birds,' in *Handbook of Social Psychology*, ed. C. Murchison (Worcester, Massachusetts: Clark University Press, 1935), pp. 947–972.

11–12. Jackdaw pecking order: Konrad Lorenz, *King Solomon's Ring*, trans. M. Kerr Wilson (London: Methuen, 1964), pp. 128–180.

12. Evolution of man: William Howells, *Mankind in the Making* (London: Pelican Books, 1967). For a more dramatic account see Robert Ardrey, *African Genesis* (London: Collins, 1961).

14. Baboon and early man: S. L. Washburn and I. De Vore, 'Social Behavior of Baboons and Early Man,' in *Social Life of Early Man*, ed. S. L. Washburn (New York: Viking, 1961), pp. 91–105. See also Robin Fox, 'In the Beginning: Aspects of Hominid Evolution,' *Man* 2 (1967): 415–433.

14–15. Baboon ecology and social behaviour: K. R. L. Hall and I. De Vore, 'Baboon Ecology' and 'Baboon Social Behavior,' *Primate Behavior*, ed. I. De Vore (New York: Holt, Rinehart and Winston, 1965), pp. 20–110.

18. Spinal cord of human community: Lionel Tiger, *Men in Groups* (London: Nelson, 1969).

18. Dominance patterns in politics: Claire Russell and W. M. S. Russell, 'An Approach to Human Ethology,' *Behavioral Science* 2, no. 3 (1957): 169–200.

18. Recent breakthroughs in the biological and social sciences: L. Tiger and R. Fox, "The Zoological Perspective in Social Science.'

19. Genetic potential of the individual and the community: Kenneth Mather, *Human Diversity* (London: Oliver and Boyd, 1964).

19. Interdependence of inborn and learned factors in human behavior: S. L. Washburn, in John Davy, 'Exploring Human Nature,' *The Observer Review*, April 20, 1969. See also G. Gaylord Simpson and Anne Roe, 'The Evolution of Behavior' in *The Behavioral Sciences Today*, ed. Berelson, pp. 94–95.

19. Socially deprived monkeys: Harry F. Harlow and M. K. Harlow, 'Social Deprivation in Monkeys,' *Scientific American*, November 1962, pp. 136–146.

20–21. Dominance fighting in street gangs: David E. Davis, 'The Phylogeny of Gangs,' in *Roots of Behavior*, ed. E. L. Bliss (New York: Harper and Row, 1962).

20–21. Artificial dominance competitions: this topic is considered more fully in Chapter 6.

NOTES TO CHAPTER 2

23. Stability of the jackdaw pecking order: Lorenz, *King Solomon's Ring*, pp. 147–148.

24. Stability of primate hierarchies: De Vore, *Primate Behavior*; Irwin S. Bernstein, 'Stability of the Status Hierarchy in a Pigtail Monkey Group (Macaca Nemestrina),' *Animal Behaviour* 17 (1969): 452–458.

25–26. Hormone treatment and habitual deference in poultry: A. M. Guhl, 'Psycho-physiological Inter-relations in the Social Behavior of Chickens,' *Psychological Bulletin* 61, no. 4 (1964): 277–285. See also A. M. Guhl, 'Social Inertia and Social Stability in Chickens,' *Animal Behaviour* 16, no. 2 (1968): 219–232.

27. Yale experiments in obedience: Stanley Milgram, 'Behavioral Study of Obedience,' *Journal of Abnormal and Social Psychology* 67, no. 4 (1963): 371–378. See also Stanley Milgram, 'Some Conditions of Obedience and Disobedience to Authority,' *Human Relations* 18 (1965): 57–76.

29. Gestapo concentration camps: Bruno Bettelheim, 'Individual and Mass Behavior in Extreme Situations,' *Journal of Abnormal and Social Psychology* 38 (1943): 417–452.

30. Soldiers under stress and patients undergoing psychotherapy: Irving Janis, 'Group Identification under Conditions of External Danger,' *British Journal of Medical Psychology* 36 (1963): 227–238.

31. Theories linking crowd psychology and hypnosis: Gustave Le Bon, *The Crowd* (New York: Viking, 1960; originally *Psychologie*

des Foules, 1895); Sigmund Freud, *Group Psychology and the Analysis of the Ego*, trans. and ed. J. Strachey (London: The Hogarth Press, 1959), in particular p. 59.

31. Prestige and hypnosis: J. C. Flugel, *Man, Morals and Society* (London: Duckworth, 1945), p. 177.

31. Freud, *Group Psychology and the Analysis of the Ego.*

31–32. The low-dominance search for a leader: we often assume that dominant leaders must be the product of their own ambition. As suggested in Chapter 4, however, they may also be capable and self-assured individuals who are content with a comparatively duty-free existence but who are pushed up into leadership positions by numbers of much less self-assured individuals who are looking for someone to whom they can relinquish control. When we do deal with the drive toward social power, it may be useful to think of it as the social aspect of a more general wish to master one's environment.

32. Brainwashing: James Moloney, 'Psychic Self-abandon and the Extortion of Confessions,' *Internal Journal of Psycho-Analysis* 36 (1955): 53–60; J. A. C. Brown, *Techniques of Persuasion* (London: Pelican Books, 1963). See also Abraham Maslow, 'Some Parallels between Sexual and Dominance Behaviour of Infra-human Primates and the Fantasies of Patients in Psychotherapy.' *Journal of Nervous and Mental Disease* 131 (1960): 202–212, in particular p. 209.

33. Psychological and physiological processes contributing to deference: we have avoided speculating on the detailed mechanics of rank order ambition and self-subordination. For the classic pschoanalytic approach see Alfred Adler, *Understanding Human Nature*, trans. W. Beran Wolfe (London: George Allen and Unwin, 1928), pp. 69–80. Additional psychoanalytic comment can be found in Erich Fromm, *Fear of Freedom* (1942; reprint ed., London: Routledge and Kegan Paul, 1960). The mechanics of psychic and emotional submission are not likely to be simple. Some hardware and software may be concerned mainly with the initial surrender, while slightly different equipment is utilized more in the long-term maintenance of the relationship (see Chapter 3 for the suggestions made by John Scott Price regarding the function of elation and depression). Of course, the relationship between the submission of a soldier to his general and the sexual submission of the female to the male would probably merit exploration.

34. Freud, *Group Psychology and the Analysis of the Ego.* For the relation between dominance and narcissism see also Philip E. Slater, 'On Social Regression,' *American Sociological Review* 28, no. 3 (June 1963): 339–364.

34–35. Dominant and dependant personality types: Abraham Maslow, 'Dominance Feeling, Behavior and Status,' *Psychological Review*, no. 44 (1937): 404–429.

35. That people can be more easily divided according to feeling than to behaviour: Maslow adds that by this he means that more can usually be predicted from the level of dominance feeling than from a measurement of past behaviour. See also Edgar Borgatta et al., 'Some Findings Relevant to the Great Man Theory of Leadership,' *American Sociological Review* 19 (1954): 755–759; Michael Argyle, *The Psychology of Interpersonal Behavior* (New York: Penguin Books, 1967), pp. 56–58.

35. Characteristic attitude of low-dominance personality: says Alfred Adler,

> People who are permeated by a spirit of servility are likewise not well adapted to positions which demand initiative. They are comfortable when they are obeying someone else's commands. The servile individual lives by the rules and laws of others, and this type seeks out a servile position almost compulsively. This servile attitude is found in the most varied of life's relationships. One can surmise its existence in the outer carriage, which usually is a somewhat bent and cringing attitude. We see them bending themselves in the presence of others, listening carefully to everyone's words, not so much to weigh and consider them, but rather to carry out their commands, and to echo and reaffirm their sentiments. They consider it an honor to appear submissive, sometimes to a perfectly unbelievable degree. (*Understanding Human Nature*, pp. 256–257.)

NOTES TO CHAPTER 3

39. The confrontation ritual in fallow deer: Konrad Lorenz, *On Aggression*, trans. M. Latzke (London: Methuen, 1966), pp. 94–98.

40. The confrontation ritual in cichlid fish: Lorenz, *On Aggression*, pp. 94–98.

40. Cat confrontations: Paul Leyhausen, 'The Communal Organisation of Solitary Mammals,' *Symposium of the Zoological Society of London* 14 (1965): 249–263.

41. Pseudo-fighting in dogs: Lorenz, *King Solomon's Ring*, pp. 186–187.

41. Evolutionary value of ritual fight: insofar as dominance decided priority in mating, there must have been a continual selection against the submissive male. This indicates the important part played by intercommunity selection in the evolution of society-dependent pseudo-fighters.

42. Gorilla confrontations: George Schaller, 'The Behavior of the Mountain Gorilla,' *Primate Behavior*, ed. De Vore, pp. 354, 363–365. See also Alex Comfort, *Nature and Human Nature* (London: Pelican Books, 1969), pp. 20–21.

43. Michael Chance's analysis: 'Social Behavior and Primate Evolution,' in *Culture and the Evolution of Man*, ed. M. F. Ashley Montague (New York: Oxford University Press, 1962), pp. 84–130.

44. Implicit physical threat in human confrontations: see Erving Goffman, *Where the Action Is* (London: Allen Lane The Penguin Press, 1969), pp. 181–196.

47. Advantage of greater size is not an absolute rule: C. K. Brain, 'Observations on the Behaviour of Vervet Monkeys (Cercopithecus Aethiops),' *Zoologica Africana* 1, no. 1: 13–27; Jerome H. Woolpy, 'The Social Organization of Wolves,' *Natural History* 77, no. 5 (1968): 46–55.

47. Dominance and fighting ability in boys' gangs: F. M. Thrasher, *The Gang, a Study of 1,313 Gangs in Chicago* (Chicago: University of Chicago Press, 1936), p. 336; William F. Whyte, *Street Corner Society* (Chicago: University of Chicago Press, 1955), p. 12. See also Ronald Lippitt et al., 'The Dynamics of Power,' *Human Relations* 5 (1952): 37–64.

48. Proper height to hold the head: many Pacific peoples hold the head sacred. This seems to be related to the erect posture dealt with in Chapter 4 as much as to the importance of height in a confrontation. There is probably a connection between the two. See Dorothy M. Spencer, 'Etiquette and Social Sanction in Fiji,' *American Anthropologist* 40 (1938): 265–266.

49. 1915 survey: see R. M. Stogdill, 'Personal Factors Associated with Leadership,' *Journal of Psychology* 25 (1948): 35–71.

49. 1943 survey: *Psychology for the Fighting Man*, 1943, pp. 373–374, quoted by Kimball Young, *Handbook of Social Psychology* (London: Routledge and Kegan Paul, 1946), p. 345.

49. 'Towering executives': Vance Packard, *The Pyramid Climbers*, (London: Longmans, 1963), p. 98.

50. Summary of research into physical size and dominance: Stogdill, 'Personal Factors Associated with Leadership.'

50. Possible childhood origin of respect for body size: Argyle, *The Psychology of Interpersonal Behavior*, p. 32.

51. Physical contact in primates: articles by Phyllis Jay, Paul E. Simonds, George Schaller, in *Primate Behavior*, ed. De Vore.

54. Personal space in a wide variety of species: Robert Ardrey, *The Territorial Imperative* (London: Collins, 1967), pp. 158–159.

54–55. Sex and the taboo against touching: Desmond Morris, *The Naked Ape* (London: Jonathan Cape, 1967), pp. 86, 185–186.

55. Edward Hall on non-verbal human communication: *The Silent*

Language (New York: Doubleday, 1959) and *The Hidden Dimension* (New York: Doubleday, 1966).

56. Roger Brown's report of his discussion with Hall: *Social Psychology* (New York: The Free Press, 1965), pp. 80–81.

56. Anxiety and personal space: Miles Patterson, 'Spatial Factors in Social Interactions,' *Human Relations* 21, no. 4 (1968): 353. See also Augustus F. Kinzel, 'Violence, the Inner Circle,' *Time Magazine*, June 6, 1969, p. 49.

56. Elbow room in transit station canteen: S. Andreski, reported by Claire and W. M. S. Russell, *Violence, Monkeys and Man* (London: Macmillan, 1968), p. 58.

57. Experiments at Groningen University: reported by T. Burns, 'Non-Verbal Communication,' *Discovery* 25, no. 10 (1964): 30–37.

59. Eye signals in primates and wolves: Brain, 'Observations on the Behaviour of Vervet Monkeys'; Woolpy, 'The Social Organization of Wolves'; articles by Phyllis Jay, Paul E. Simonds, and George Schaller in *Primate Behavior*, ed. De Vore.

59. Freud on hypnotist's eyes: *Group Psychology and the Analysis of the Ego*, p. 57.

59. Evil Eye: Edward S. Gifford, *The Evil Eye*, reported by S. Tomkins in *Affect, Imagery, Consciousness* (New York: Springer Publishing, 1963), pp. 159–160.

61–62. Eye contact experiments: reported by Michael Argyle, *The Psychology of Interpersonal Behavior*, pp. 105–115.

62. Eye space in turkeys: Glen McBride, *A General Theory of Social Behaviour* (St. Lucia: University of Queensland Press, 1964).

65. Schjelderup-Ebbe's observations on bird behaviour: 'Social Behavior of Birds.'

66. 'It is difficult to think …': John S. Price, 'The Dominance Hierarchy and the Evolution of Mental Illness,' *Lancet*, no. 2 (1967): 243–246.

66–67. 'He becomes depressed …': John S. Price, 'The Ritualization of Agonistic Behaviour as a Determinant of Variation along the Neuroticism/Stability Dimension of Personality,' abridged in *Proceedings of the Royal Society of Medicine* 62 (November 1969): 1107–1110.

NOTES TO CHAPTER 4

70. Cat establishments: Leyhausen, 'The Communal Organisation of Solitary Mammals.'

70. Cats in confinement: Charles Winslow, 'Observations of Dominance—Subordination in Cats,' *Journal of Genetic Psychology* 52 (1938): 425–428.

70–71. Dominant bearing in monkeys: Abraham Maslow, 'The Role of Dominance in the Social and Sexual Behavior of Infra-human Primates: Part I,' *Journal of Genetic Psychology* 48 (1936): 261–277, in particular p. 266.

71. 'Delinquency strut' and *sandunga*: Goffman, *Where the Action Is*, p. 191.

71–72. Jackdaw threat postures: Lorenz, *King Solomon's Ring*, p. 164.

72. Human high-dominance bearing: Abraham Maslow: Dominance Feeling. Behaviour and Status'; Jurgen Ruesch and Weldon Kees, *Non-Verbal Communication* (Berkeley and Los Angeles: University of California Press, 1956), p. 38. For dominant and subordinate bearing in primitive societies see the following:

Fiji: 'When others are seated in the room it is polite when moving about to *yato vasewa*, or to "walk small," that is, in a stooping position. Women, if they wish to move around when men are seated in the house, do so by crawling on their hands and knees.' (Dorothy M. Spencer, 'Etiquette and Social Sanction in Fiji.')

Kwakiutl: Margaret Mead, *Co-operation and Competition among Primitive Peoples* (Boston: Beacon Press, 1961), p. 192.

Trobriand islanders: 'One of the main sociological features at once strikes an observant newcomer—the existence of rank and social differentiation. Some of the natives—very frequently those of the finer looking type—are treated with most marked deference by others, and in return, these chiefs and persons of rank behave in a quite different way to the strangers. In fact, they show excellent manners in the full meaning of the word.

'When a chief is present, no commoner dares to remain in a physically higher position; he has to bend his body or squat. Similarly, when a chief sits down, no one would dare to stand.' [Bronislaw Malinowski, *Argonauts of the Western Pacific* (London: Routledge, 1922), p. 52.]

73. Chimpanzee militancy: Lorenz, *On Aggression*, pp. 231–232.

76–77. Uganda chimpanzees: Vernon and Frances Reynolds, 'Chimpanzees of the Budongo Forest,' *Primate Behavior*, ed. De Vore; Vernon Reynolds, *The Apes* (London: Cassell, 1968), p. 128.

77. 'The most dominant rooster ...': Carl Murchison, 'The Experimental Measurement of a Social Hierarchy in *Gallus Domesticus*: Part III,' *Journal of Genetic Psychology*, no. 46 (1935): 76–101, in particular pp. 100–101.

77. Relaxed manner expected of human leaders: W. M. S. and Claire Russell, *Human Behaviour: A New Approach* (London: Deutsch, 1961), pp. 144, 149.

77. Slow speaking and leadership ability: Office of Strategic Services, *The Assessment of Men* (New York: Rinehart, 1968), p. 304.

78. 'In analysis of the walking ...': Philip Eisenberg, 'Expressive

Movements Related to Feeling of Dominance,' *Archives of Psychology*, ed. R. S. Woodworth, no. 211 (New York: Columbia University, May 1937), p. 58.

79. 'Umbrella of the myriad people': J. Macgowan, *Men and Manners of Modern China* (London: Unwin, 1912), pp. 302–304.

79–80. Chinese face: Hsien Chin Hu, 'The Chinese Concepts of Face,' *American Anthropologist* 46 (1944), pp. 45–64.

83. Concept of face among North American Indians: see Marcel Mauss, *The Gift*, trans. I. Cunnison (London: Cohen and West, 1969), p. 38. Modern Western interpretation of face: Erving Goffman, 'On Face-Work: An Analysis of Ritual Elements in Social Interaction,' *Psychiatry* 18, no. 3 (August 1955): 213–231 (expanded in Goffman, *Where the Action Is*).

83. 'I am the first of the tribes ...': Ruth Benedict, *Patterns of Culture* (1935; reprint ed., London: Routledge and Kegan Paul, 1968), p. 138.

83. 'I am powerful ...': in *Ancient Records of Assyria and Babylon*, trans. D. D. Luckenbill (Chicago: University of Chicago Press, 1926), vol. 2.

86. Definition of the situation: Erving Goffman, *The Presentation of Self in Everyday Life* (London: Allen Lane The Penguin Press, 1969).

90. Role playing: Goffman, *Where the Action Is*, and *The Presentation of Self in Everyday Life*; Michael Banton, *Roles* (London: Tavistock Publications, 1965).

91. Samoan 'talking chief': this topic is considered more fully in Chapter 6.

95. 'Like the jester of old ...': Thrasher, *The Gang, a Study of 1,313 Gangs in Chicago*, pp. 337–338.

95. Court buffoon: Enid Welsford, *The Fool, His Social and Literary History* (London: Faber and Faber, 1935).

99. Talking time 'pecking orders': Argyle, *The Psychology of Interpersonal Behavior*, p. 70.

101. Instinctive signalling systems: N. Tinbergen, *The Study of Instinct* (Oxford: Clarendon Press, 1951) and *Social Behaviour in Animals* (London: Methuen, 1953).

101–102. Chinese face: Hsien Chin Hu, 'The Chinese Concepts of Face.'

NOTES TO CHAPTER 5

109. Aztec class divisions: J. Soustelle, *Daily Life of the Aztecs*, trans. P. O'Brian (London: Pelican Books, 1964), pp. 57–108.

113. Class distinctions in dress in ancient Egypt: James Laver, *A Concise History of Costume* (London: Thames and Hudson, 1969),

p. 16. See also Barbara Mertz, *Red Land, Black Land* (London: Hodder and Stoughton, 1967), pp. 85–93.

113. Clothing regulations in medieval Europe: James Laver, *Clothes* (London: Burke, 1952), pp. 39–50.

114. Class distinctions in dress in China (T'ang): Jacques Gernet, *Daily Life in China on the Eve of the Mongol Invasions, 1250–1276* (London: Allen and Unwin, 1962), p. 128.

114. Class distinctions in dress in Aztec Mexico: Soustelle, *Daily Life of the Aztecs*, pp. 138–148, in particular pp. 147–148.

115. Class distinctions in Japan: Ruth Benedict, *The Chrysanthemum and the Sword* (Boston: Houghton Mifflin, 1946).

115. Class distinctions in the Inca Empire: R. L. Beals and H. Hoijer, *An Introduction to Anthropology*, 3rd ed. (New York: Macmillan, 1965), pp. 559–561.

116. Japanese respect language: Benedict, *The Chrysanthemum and the Sword*.

116–117. Aztec speech: Soustelle, *Daily Life of the Aztecs*, pp. 225–226.

117. Modern Malay: Margaret Schlauch, *The Gift of Tongues* (London: George Allen and Unwin, 1943), p. 271.

118. George Bernard Shaw: *Pygmalion*.

120–122. Aztec education: Soustelle, *Daily Life of the Aztecs*, pp. 223–230 ('Never forget that you descend ...': p. 149; 'One must speak calmly ...': p. 224; 'walk quietly ...': p. 224).

125. The English public school: Rupert Wilkinson, *The Prefects* (London: Oxford University Press, 1964) ('a mysterious aura of differentness ...': p. 13). See also E. Wingfield-Statford, *The Making of a Gentleman* (London: Williams and Norgate, 1938), pp. 295–310.

126. 'Mystical glamour and lordly attitude': Joseph Schumpeter, quoted by Rupert Wilkinson, *The Prefects*, p. 13.

127–128. 'The school possessed the biggest ...': Winston Churchill, *My Early Life* (London: Odhams Press, 1947), pp. 17–18.

129. Inevitable development of the class system: the class system frequently developed in surprisingly small communities as a result of tribal conquest. However, its greatest historical importance appears to stem from its ordering effect in large communities where for thousands of years no other ranking technique could compete with it.

132–134. Indian caste system: Jeanine Auboyer, *Daily Life in Ancient India*, trans. S. Watson Taylor (London: Weidenfeld and Nicolson, 1965), pp. 21–37.

134–35. 'Servitude is ordained by God ...': school of St. Anselm of Laon (early twelfth century), quoted by R. W. Southern, *The Making of the Middle Ages* (London: Hutchinson, 1953), p. 104.

135. Eight thousand killed in duels between 1589 and 1608: *Encyclopaedia Britannica*, 1969 ed. s.v. 'Duel.'
135. Francis de Montmorency at his execution: Robert Baldick, *The Duel* (London: Chapman and Hall, 1965), pp. 57–58.
136. Ralph Linton on lower caste Hindus: *The Study of Man* (New York: D. Appleton-Century, 1936), p. 131.

NOTES TO CHAPTER 6

140. Eskimo song contests: E. A. Hoebel, 'Law and the Social Order,' in *Anthropology*, ed. S. Rapport and H. Wright (London: University of London Press, 1967), pp. 195–212.
140–41. Crow battle honours: Beals and Hoijer, *An Introduction to Anthropology*, p. 548.
141. Germanic battle honours: Tacitus extract (trans. A. J. Church and W. J. Brodribb) in *Primitive Heritage*, ed. M. Mead and N. Calas (London: Victor Gollancz, 1954), pp. 8–12. For the extent to which this social pattern continued to influence life in the Christian era see Dorothy Whitelock, *The Beginnings of English Society* (London: Pelican Books, 1952), pp. 27–35, 57.
143. Samoan ranking system: Beals and Hoijer, *An Introduction to Anthropology*, pp. 551–553; Mead, *Co-operation and Competition among Primitive Peoples*, pp. 282–312, and *Coming of Age in Samoa* (1928; reprint ed., London: Penguin Books, 1969); Felix M. Keesing, assist. M. M. Keesing, 'Elite Communication in Samoa, A Study of Leadership,' in *Culture Change*, ed. Felix M. Keesing (Stanford: Stanford University Press, 1952).
144–45. Manus ranking system: Margaret Mead, *Co-operation and Competition among Primitive Peoples*, pp. 210–239, and *Growing Up in New Guinea* (1930; reprint ed., London: Pelican Books, 1968). Margaret Mead records the great change the Manus have subsequently undergone in *New Lives For Old* (London: Victor Gollancz, 1956).
145. 'Rubbish men': it is difficult for us to appreciate what an extremely derogatory term this must be among the Manus, where property is even more jealously guarded than in our own society. To pick up a banana floating near somebody else's house is to be a thief. No useful property is ever wasted by the Manus, hence the word rubbish, when applied to men, is a far stronger insult (Mead, *Growing Up in New Guinea*, pp. 31–33).
146. Zuni Indians: Benedict, *Patterns of Culture*, pp. 57–129.
146. Arapesh of New Guinea: Mead, *Co-operation and Competition among Primitive Peoples*, pp. 20–50.
146–50. Kwakiutl ranking system: Mead, *Co-operation and Competition among Primitive Peoples*, pp. 180–209; Benedict, *Patterns*

of *Culture*, pp. 173–221; Franz Boas, 'Social Organization of the Kwakiutl,' *American Anthropologist* 22 (1920): 111–126; H. G. Barnett, 'The Nature of the Potlatch,' *American Anthropologist* 40 (1938): 349–358; Helen Codere, *Fighting with Property* (New York: J. J. Augustin, 1950) and 'Kwakiutl Society—Rank without Class,' *American Anthropologist* 59 (1957): 473–486. For Kwakiutl face and the dancing mask see Marcel Mauss, *The Gift*, p. 38.

150. 'He wasn't sick at all …': Codere, *Fighting with Property*, p. 77.

151. Logic of potlatch compared to modern exchange of 'treats': Barnett, 'The Nature of the Potlatch'; C. Levi-Strauss, *The Elementary Structures of Kinship*, trans. J. H. Bell and J. R. von Sturmer (London: Tavistock, 1970), pp. 56–57.

152. Recipe for success in American business world: Vance Packard, *The Pyramid Climbers*, Chap. 13.

156. Private ownership in primitive societies: for example see Chapter 6, n. 145 above.

157. Commercial class suppression in Aztec Mexico: Soustelle, *Daily Life of the Aztecs*, pp. 77–83.

158. Contempt for 'trade' in China: Wilkinson, *The Prefects*, p. 137.

161. Kwakiutl religious beliefs and folk-tales: Benedict, *Patterns of Culture* ('When calamities are prolonged …': p. 159).

162. Medieval life and dogma: Southern, *The Making of the Middle Ages*.

164. Commercial power and the Reformation: R. H. Tawney, *Religion and the Rise of Capitalism* (London: John Murray, 1926); Max Weber, *The Protestant Ethic and the Spirit of Capitalism*, trans. Talcott Parsons (London: George Allen and Unwin, 1930). On the Protestant sanctification of money: Franz Steiner, 'Notes on Comparative Economics,' *British Journal of Sociology* 5, no. 2 (1954): 118–129.

168–69. Competitive largesse in primitive societies: Marcel Mauss, *The Gift*.

INDEX

Adler, Alfred, 20
Adolescence, 20–1
  hierarchy formation in, 20–1
   139
  posture of, 75
  street gangs of, 21, 47
  See also Children *and* Education
Agricultural society, 106, 130
  See also Tribal societies *and specific societies*
Amery, Leopold, 127–8
Animal societies *see specific animal society*
Ants, 19
Ape societies, 12–14
  See also Chimpanzee society *and* Gorilla society
Arapesh society, 145
Arguer role, 96–100
Argyle, Michael, 62
Aristocrats, 105
  bearing of, 73
  education of, 105–6, 109–11, 118–19, 121–2, 124–9
  sports of, 121
  See also Hereditary class-ranking system
Army, 25, 29–32
  in hereditary class-ranking system, 109
  institutionalized rank order in, 16
  leader idealization in, 30
  officer hierarchy in, 142–3
  posture in, 73
Aztec Empire
  class defences in, 157–8
  clothing dominance, signals of, 114–15
  compulsory education in, 120–1, 128
  masculine ideal in, 121–2

respect language (Nahuatl) of, 116–17
  sports in, 121

Baboon society, 13–16
  co-operation in, 14, 15–16
  deference shown in, 14, 29, 53
  social grooming in, 14–15, 33, 91
  social responsibility in, 15–16
  stability of, 15, 23, 26
  tyranny in, 13, 14, 26
Bees, 19
Bettelheim, Bruno, 29–30
Bird societies, 19
  See also specific bird societies
Boasting, 82–5, 96, 99–100
Body contact, 50–3, 69
Body size, 46–50, 69
Bonaparte, Napoleon, 49
Bouteville, comte de (Francis de Montmorency), 135
Bowing (human), 14, 55
Bragging, 82–5, 96, 99–100
Brahmans (Indian caste), 132–4
Brainwashing, 32
Broadside display, 39, 40, 42
Brown, Roger, 55–6
Buddhism, 134
Business organization, 16
  See also Industrial ranking system

Caged communities, 10–11, 23–4, 53–4
Caste system (Indian), 132–4
Cats, domestic
  bearing of, 70
  confrontation behaviour, 40–1
Chance, Michael, 43, 54
Children
  body-size sensitivity and, 50.

Fontana Social Science

Books available include:

African Genesis Robert Ardrey **50p**

The Territorial Imperative Robert Ardrey **50p**

Racial Minorities Michael Banton **50p**

The Sociology of Modern Britain
Edited by Eric Butterworth and David Weir **60p**

Social Problems of Modern Britain
Edited by Eric Butterworth and David Weir **75p**

Strikes Richard Hyman **50p**

Memories, Dreams, Reflections C. J. Jung **60p**

Strike at Pilkingtons Tony Lane and Kenneth Roberts **50p**

Figuring Out Society Ronald Meek **45p**

Lectures on Economic Principles Sir Dennis Robertson **75p**

People and Cities Stephen Verney **37½p**

Fontana Politics

Books available include:

Battle for the Environment Tony Aldous **45p**

The English Constitution Walter Bagehot
Edited by R. H. S. Crossman **40p**

War in Modern Society Alastair Buchan **42½p**

At War With Asia Noam Chomsky **50p**

Problems of Knowledge and Freedom Noam Chomsky **30p**

Selected Writings of Mahatma Gandhi
Edited by Ronald Duncan **45p**

Marx and Engels: Basic Writings
Edited by Lewis S. Feuer **50p**

Governing Britain A. H. Hanson and Malcolm Walles **50p**

The Commons in Transition *Edited by* A. H. Hanson and
Bernard Crick **50p**

Sir Charles Dilke Roy Jenkins **52½p**

Europe Tomorrow *Edited by* Richard Mayne **60p**

Machiavelli: Selections *Edited by* John Plamenatz **60p**

Democracy in America Alexis de Tocqueville
Edited by J. P. Mayer and Max Lerner Vols I & II **75p each**

The Cabinet Patrick Gordon Walker **40p**

The Downfall of the Liberal Party 1914–1935
Trevor Wilson **60p**

Economics and Policy Donald Winch **80p**